MW00834883

Written Corrective Feedback for
L2 Development

SECOND LANGUAGE ACQUISITION

Series Editors: **Professor David Singleton**, *University of Pannonia, Hungary* and Fellow Emeritus, *Trinity College, Dublin, Ireland* and **Dr Simone E. Pfenninger**, *University of Zurich, Switzerland*

This series brings together titles dealing with a variety of aspects of language acquisition and processing in situations where a language or languages other than the native language is involved. Second language is thus interpreted in its broadest possible sense. The volumes included in the series all offer in their different ways, on the one hand, exposition and discussion of empirical findings and, on the other, some degree of theoretical reflection. In this latter connection, no particular theoretical stance is privileged in the series; nor is any relevant perspective – sociolinguistic, psycholinguistic, neurolinguistic, etc. – deemed out of place. The intended readership of the series includes final-year undergraduates working on second language acquisition projects, postgraduate students involved in second language acquisition research, and researchers and teachers in general whose interests include a second language acquisition component.

Full details of all the books in this series and of all our other publications can be found on http://www.multilingual-matters.com, or by writing to Multilingual Matters, St Nicholas House, 31-34 High Street, Bristol BS1 2AW, UK.

SECOND LANGUAGE ACQUISITION: 96

Written Corrective Feedback for L2 Development

John Bitchener and Neomy Storch

MULTILINGUAL MATTERS
Bristol • Buffalo • Toronto

Library of Congress Cataloging in Publication Data
A catalog record for this book is available from the Library of Congress.
Bitchener, John, author. | Storch, Neomy, author.
Written Corrective Feedback for L2 Development/John Bitchener and Neomy Storch.
Bristol; Buffalo: Multilingual Matters, [2016] |
Second Language Acquisition: 96 | Includes bibliographical references and index.
LCCN 2015036354| ISBN 9781783095049 (hbk : alk. paper) | ISBN 9781783095032
(pbk : alk. paper) | ISBN 9781783095056 (ebook)
LCSH: Second language acquisition. | Written communication. | Language and languages–
Study and teaching.
LCC P118.2 .B555 2016 | DDC 418.0071–dc23 LC record available at http://lccn.loc.
gov/2015036354

British Library Cataloguing in Publication Data
A catalogue entry for this book is available from the British Library.

ISBN-13: 978-1-78309-504-9 (hbk)
ISBN-13: 978-1-78309-503-2 (pbk)

Multilingual Matters
UK: St Nicholas House, 31-34 High Street, Bristol BS1 2AW, UK.
USA: UTP, 2250 Military Road, Tonawanda, NY 14150, USA.
Canada: UTP, 5201 Dufferin Street, North York, Ontario M3H 5T8, Canada.

Website: www.multilingual-matters.com
Twitter: Multi_Ling_Mat
Facebook: https://www.facebook.com/multilingualmatters
Blog: www.channelviewpublications.wordpress.com

The policy of Multilingual Matters/Channel View Publications is to use papers that
are natural, renewable and recyclable products, made from wood grown in sustainable
forests. In the manufacturing process of our books, and to further support our policy,
preference is given to printers that have FSC and PEFC Chain of Custody certification.
The FSC and/or PEFC logos will appear on those books where full certification has been
granted to the printer concerned.

Typeset by Deanta Global Publishing Services Limited.
Printed and bound by CPI Group (UK) Ltd, Croydon, CR0 4YY

Contents

Acknowledgements

John's acknowledgements I am extremely grateful to a number of people who have stimulated my thinking on the role of written CF for L2 development and to those who have provided feedback on both draft iterations and oral presentations of sections of the work presented in this book. Among such contributors, I wish to thank Dr Shaofeng Li (University of Auckland) for his thoughtful comments on the first draft of Chapter 2 and to a number of international colleagues who provided oral feedback in personal exchanges and during oral presentations of the work during my recent sabbatical travels: Professors Lourdes Ortega, Heidi Byrnes (Georgetown University), Professor Charlene Polio (Michigan State University), Dr Jenifer Philp (Lancaster University) and Dr Andrea Revesz (University of London). Without the financial support of my university (AUT University), access to these colleagues would not have been possible. In recent years, my thinking has also been stimulated by PhD students working on written CF projects and to each of these people, I offer a huge amount of thanks for the conversations we have had on the potential of written CF: Stephanie Rummel, Qi Guo, Saeed Roshan and Su Li. On a personal level, I am ever grateful to the support and encouragement of my partner, Edwin Cheong, and my parents, John and Marjorie Bitchener. Last, but not least, I wish to thank my co-author, Neomy Storch, for agreeing to join me in the writing of this book.

Neomy's acknowledgements I would like to acknowledge the feedback I received from Professor Merrill Swain on earlier drafts of the chapters on sociocultural theory. Her insights, as always, were invaluable. I would also like to thank Marzooq Aldossary, my PhD student, for his creativity in drawing the figures included in the book. I would like to thank Tim McNamara, Janne Morton and Celia Thompson, my dear colleagues at Melbourne University, for their continuous encouragement and moral support. Finally, I would like to thank my family, and particularly the men in my life: my husband Paul, and my sons Amir and Edan, for their love and support throughout my academic career.

The authors and publishers are grateful to Wiley for giving permission to reproduce two figures of copyright materials. Figure 5.1 is a reproduction of the figure that appeared on p. 471 in the work of Aljaafreh, A. & Lantolf, J.P. (1994). Negative feedback as regulation and second language learning in the zone of proximal development. Published in the *Modern Language Journal, 78*, 465–483. Figure 5.2 is a reproduction of the figure that appeared on p. 209 in the work of Lee, I. (2014). Revising teacher feedback in EFL writing from sociocultural perspectives. *TESOL Quarterly*, 48, 201–2013.

Joint acknowledgements We are both extremely grateful for the support and guidance of our editor at Multilingual Matters, Laura Longworth, and the entire editorial and production team. We are also appreciative of the anonymous reviewers' detailed and stimulating suggestions. Last but not least, we would like to thank Qi Guo (Christina) for the excellent work she did with creating our index.

1 Introduction

1.0 The Aim of the Book

The overarching aim of the book is to consider from two theoretical and empirical perspectives (cognitive and sociocultural) the potential of written CF to facilitate L2 development and some of the factors that may explain why written CF may or may not lead to L2 development. Thus, our focus is on the learning of the L2 rather than on the editing of L2 writing for composition and other such purposes.

We begin our discussion of this chapter (Section 1.1) with a consideration of the two key terms referred to in the aim: **written CF** and **L2 development**. This is followed by a discussion of the importance of written CF for L2 development (Section 1.2) and an outline of the structure and focus of Chapters 2–6 (Section 1.3).

1.1 Defining Key Terms

1.1.1 Written CF

Written CF is a written response to a linguistic error that has been made in the writing of a text by an L2 learner. It seeks to either correct the inaccurate usage or provide information about where the error has occurred and/or about the cause of the error and how it may be corrected. If the focus is on correcting the error, the response will be in the form of a direct error correction. If the focus is on locating the error so that the learner can then attempt to correct it, an indirect response will be given. Typically, this will be provided as an underlining or circling of the error or by means of a line-by-line error tally in the margin of the text. As the third type of response, meta-linguistic information (e.g. explanations/ rules and examples of correct usage) may be provided to help the learner understand why the error has occurred and how to correct it. Sometimes the meta-linguistic feedback may be in the form of a code (e.g. PT for Past Tense error). It is generally understood that written CF is provided on linguistic errors rather than on content or organisational errors or issues. Most frequently, it has tended to focus on grammatical errors but it can also be provided on lexical and non-grammatical errors (e.g. punctuation, spelling). Most L2 learners receive written CF from their language class teachers but sometimes they also receive it from native and more advanced non-native speakers outside the language classroom or from their peers in peer response activities. Although written CF has traditionally been delivered on hard paper copies of students' texts, accompanied at times by oral face-to-face conferences, it is increasingly being delivered electronically via synchronous or asynchronous modes of communication and by means of a range of web-based commenting software.

1.1.2   L2 development

L2 development is about the processes and stages involved in developing knowledge of the L2 and about how to use it accurately as a native speaker/writer or a near native speaker/writer would be expected to use it. The development process begins immediately after some form of L2 information input (in this case, by means of written CF) has been provided and may continue for months or years, depending on the goals, proficiency and mastery of the L2 learner.

Sometimes the construct **L2 development** is used interchangeably with **L2 learning** and **L2 acquisition** but, in purist terms, each has its own particular focus or shade of meaning. The choice of terms may also depend on the theoretical perspective it is situated within (see discussion in Chapter 4). **L2 learning** and **L2 development** are most often used interchangeably to refer to the process or processes of learning from the learner's perspective even though the term **L2 development** is, arguably, more about specific stages in the learning process. **L2 acquisition** can be understood in terms of either the acquired end-product (native speaker mastery and competence) or the process of acquiring the L2 and, in this regard, is similar to the process of **L2 learning** and **L2 development**.

In this book, we use the term **L2 development** because we believe it is a more precise term, namely, one that includes reference to any or all of the stages in the development of the L2, from the initial written CF input stage to the implicit, automatised output stage. From a sociocultural perspective, progress also includes a greater ability to self-correct. It is important to note that progress may not always be linear and forward-moving; it may sometimes involve small steps, both forwards and backwards, in the processing and use of the feedback.

Relating these definitions/explanations to the central aim of the book, it can be seen that our focus is on understanding whether or not written CF, in any of its forms, has the potential to facilitate L2 development over time. To understand its potential, we examine, in Chapters 2 and 4, the two theoretical perspectives on how and why written CF might be able to target L2 errors and facilitate development. Then, in Chapters 3 and 5, we review the empirical research to see whether or not, and the extent to which, written CF has been found to assist L2 development. In our examination of the extent of its effectiveness, we consider not only the cognitive processing conditions but also the context-related and individual learner factors or variables that have been hypothesised and shown to facilitate or impede the effectiveness of written CF for L2 development. Before we outline the focus of each Chapter, we discuss the importance of written CF as a topic of investigation.

1.2   The Importance of Written CF for L2 Development

A number of reasons can be given for discussing the potential of written CF for L2 development. The first concerns the amount of time that many language teachers spend correcting the written errors that their students make. Although some teachers do not agree that written CF is necessary or effective, most do, to some extent at least. Those who are sceptical of its value tend to base this view on their observations of students who fail to respond to the feedback they are given or who fail to retain over time the knowledge they appear to have gained immediately after feedback has been provided (as evident in revised and/or new texts). Nevertheless, many teachers are of the view that some of their students will benefit from some of the feedback they receive on some occasions at least, and that some improvement is better than no improvement or no opportunity for improvement. Thus, from a pedagogical perspective, questions concerning the potential of written CF for L2 development and factors that may facilitate and/or impede the development process are of interest and importance to teachers who want to know whether their practices are likely to benefit their learners' development.

Although most teachers assume, to some extent at least, that giving their students written CF contributes to the learning process in some way (Ferris, 2003), Truscott's (1996) call for the abandonment of the practice challenged these assumptions. He argued that there was no compelling research evidence of the benefits of written CF for L2 development. The studies he referred to as evidence were limited to four (see Chapter 3) and, as a number of critics (e.g. Bitchener & Ferris, 2012; Ferris, 1999; Guenette, 2007; Van Beuningen et al., 2012) have explained, the validity and reliability of the findings of these studies as evidence should be questioned. He also claimed that there are conflicting theoretical views (see Chapter 2 for detail) about whether one could even expect written CF to facilitate such development. The controversy (see Ferris, 1999, 2004, 2010; Truscott, 1996, 1999, 2004, 2009) arising from this call did, however, lead to a number of theoretical discussions in the literature (see Chapter 2 and articles in *Studies in Second Language Acquisition* Special Issue, volume 32, and in *Journal of Second Language Acquisition* Special Issue, volume 21) about whether one could expect written CF to be effective as a means of facilitating L2 development. Overall, the claims made by

Truscott (1996) did the field a service insofar as they led to research about the key questions of concern to teachers, theorists and researchers that had not been satisfactorily answered:

(1) Can written CF facilitate L2 development (measured in terms of the improved written accuracy of L2 learners)?
(2) Are more explicit types of written CF (e.g. indirect forms, direct error correction, meta-linguistic information) more effective than other types?
(3) Can written CF facilitate the learning of some linguistic forms/ structures more than others?
(4) Is written CF more effective if it is focused (i.e. targets one or only a few forms/structures at a time) or unfocused (i.e. comprehensive)?
(5) Do some individual and contextual factors moderate the effectiveness of written CF more than others?

These questions, in one form or other, became the focus of most of the empirical studies situated within the cognitive perspective and tended to be more pedagogically motivated than theoretically motivated. They were more about whether written CF 'worked' (i.e. whether improved accuracy resulted from the feedback when measured in text revisions and new written texts) than about why and how it 'worked' or did not 'work'. The focus was more on the revised output (the product) than on the cognitive processing of the feedback.

Another important reason for our focus on the contribution of written CF to L2 development is the fact that the feedback is **written**, that is, it relates to errors occurring in the written texts of L2 learners rather than to those occurring in their oral interactions. Until recently, second language acquisition (SLA) accounts of L2 learning have been more focused on acquired competence, namely, the consistent, implicit, automatised use of the target language, situated in the online, oral medium. Theorists and researchers (e.g. Bitchener, 2012; Polio, 2012; Williams, 2012) have already pointed out what they see as crucial advantages for L2 development if learners are given opportunities to write and receive written CF on the linguistic accuracy of their written texts. The first advantage concerns the permanence of the written text. Having written CF on a written text means that learners can refer to the feedback as often as they wish, whereas, in oral communication, the spoken utterance and any feedback received is fleeting and unable to be referred to again. Another advantage is the additional time that learners have to draw upon their stored L2 knowledge in their long-term memory and consider it in relation to the information provided in the written CF before hypothesising the correct L2 form/structure to use.

It is understandable that writing and written CF have tended to be the poor cousin of oral communication and oral CF when it comes to understanding the role they may play in the learning process. Because oral communication is delivered and received under online conditions, it is more likely, more often, to draw on the learner's implicit, automatised knowledge and, therefore, to be a potentially more reliable indicator of what the learner has acquired. However, this does not necessarily mean that, in terms of feedback, oral CF is any more effective than written CF. For learners to progress through the various information-processing stages (discussed in Chapter 2) and then consolidate what they have learnt from written CF over time, written CF would seem, theoretically, to be better able to help learners develop their explicit, conscious knowledge of the L2 in the early stages of development.

Thus, there are a number of reasons for writing a book that focuses on a traditionally popular pedagogical practice (written CF) and on one that has been relatively ignored in terms of its contribution to L2 development.

1.3 The Structure and Focus of Chapters 2–6

1.3.1 Chapter 2

In Chapter 2, we present a theoretical case or argument in support of the view that written CF has the potential to facilitate L2 development. This case is situated within a cognitive perspective and draws upon what SLA theories and hypotheses say about the nature and conditions of cognitively processing L2 information, including that provided by written CF. It explains how and why written CF has the potential to contribute to the development of a learner's L2 knowledge and use.

The argument begins by stating that the central goal of L2 learning is the acquisition of native or near native speaker competence. Given that there are two types of linguistic competence (acquired and learnt), we explain that the goal of acquired competence (which draws upon implicit knowledge, accessed automatically and without conscious reflection) can be developed from learnt competence (which draws upon explicit input such as that provided by explicit written CF). To explain how this process works, we draw upon the skill acquisition theories and models of Anderson (1976, 1980, 1983, 1993) and McLaughlin (1978, 1980, 1987, 1990), because they explain how explicit/declarative L2 knowledge can be proceduralised through meaningful, contextualised practice (DeKeyser, 2007) over time, to a point where it may be converted to implicit, acquired knowledge. Then, we describe the conscious information-processing stages and conditions that have been identified by cognitive/interactionist theorists (e.g. Schmidt, 1990, 1994, 2001; Tomlin & Villa, 1994) from the point where learners are provided with written CF as input on their linguistic error(s) to the point where they are able to accurately modify the errors and produce new texts devoid of the errors. We refer to the framework of a single written CF episode, designed by Gass (1997), to explain the five stages in the processing of new knowledge: input (written CF) is provided; attention is given to the written CF input; noticing and understanding the difference between the written CF input and the linguistic error it refers to; internalising and integrating the written CF as input. We explain that producing accurate written output, as a result of this conscious processing, is the beginning of a longer consolidation process during which appropriately contextualised practice may facilitate acquired competence. Because this model only explains an idealised information-processing route, we conclude the chapter with a discussion of the factors or variables that might interrupt the development process (1) at any of the stages identified in the Gass (1997) framework and (2) at any stage in the retrieval and processing of new knowledge during the on-going consolidation phase. We consider, for example, individual internal factors (cognitive and affective) and individual external factors (contextual/social/pedagogical).

1.3.2 Chapter 3

In this chapter, we critically review the research on written CF that has been conducted within the cognitive perspective, in order to determine its contribution to L2 development. This body of research has been guided by the five overarching questions referred to earlier in Section 1.2. It would be fair to say that the questions have been more pedagogically motivated than theoretically motivated (Bitchener, 2012; Polio, 2012), and have therefore tended to focus more on the end-product of processing each episode of written CF input. In other words, the focus has been on whether explicit feedback has facilitated a significant improvement in accuracy on certain occasions (immediately after the feedback has been provided and on subsequent occasions over time). In terms of investigating why learners improve or fail to improve their written accuracy on such occasions, most of the research, it will be seen, has not followed this line of investigation. The information-processing stages and conditions discussed in Chapter 2 have not been the primary focus of the written CF studies until more recently. Thus, it will be seen that many of the theoretical explanations outlined in Chapter 2 have not been the focus of empirical investigations. As a result, there has tended to be something of a disconnect between the theoretical and empirical foci. Nevertheless, many studies have drawn to some extent on some theoretical explanations to account for their findings. So, while theoretical explanations have generally not guided the design of research questions until quite recently, they have, at times, been drawn upon in a relatively ad hoc manner to explain why various findings may have occurred. By the end of our review, we are in a position to comment on the extent to which the research currently available has been able to explain why written CF may be effective in facilitating L2 development.

1.3.3   Chapter 4

In Chapter 4, we introduce sociocultural theory (SCT), a theory based on the work of Vygotsky (1978, 1981) which has been applied to L2 learning and teaching by scholars such as Lantolf (e.g. Lantolf, 2000; Lantolf & Thorne, 2006) and Swain (e.g. Swain, 2000, 2010). Unlike cognitive theories discussed above, SCT views all cognitive development, including L2 development, as inherently social rather than cognitive. Thus, its main focus is on the nature of human behaviour in social interaction. We begin with an overview of the theory, noting also how it differs in its conceptualisation of learning processes and in approaches to research from cognitive perspectives. We then focus our discussion on some key and interrelated constructs in the theory that are of pertinence to a discussion of written CF: (a) the Zone of Proximal Development (ZPD) and scaffolding, (b) mediation and tools, and (c) the notion of activity. We first explain what these constructs mean and then how they may explain why written CF may or may not lead to L2 development.

We begin by noting that SCT assigns interaction between an expert (e.g. teacher, peer) and a novice (e.g. language learner) a central role in human cognitive development. Development depends, however, on the appropriate form of assistance. Appropriate assistance needs to take into consideration the learner's current and potential levels of competence (the ZPD), and responds to the learner's evolving competence. This negotiated and responsive form of assistance is referred to as scaffolding. We suggest that written CF is a form of assistance with a potential to lead to L2 development but, for that potential to be realised, the feedback needs to be a form of scaffolded assistance. We thus proceed to discuss the key attributes of scaffolded written CF.

We then discuss the constructs of mediation and tools in SCT, distinguishing between material (e.g. computers) and symbolic (e.g. language) tools. These tools can affect the nature of the written CF (quantity and quality of the comments) and, more importantly perhaps, how learners engage with that feedback. It is the quality of learners' engagement with the written CF that may help explain why feedback results in L2 development. In discussing language as a tool, we draw mainly on the work of Swain (2006a, 2010) and her notion of **languaging**; that is, using language when discussing or thinking through solutions to problems. Language enables the expert and novice to communicate and to co-construct appropriate forms of scaffolded feedback. Language also enables the learner to process and internalise the feedback.

The final section of this chapter considers how we can explain learners' response to written CF; that is, whether and how they engage with the feedback, by viewing feedback as an activity which takes place in a particular context. The notion of activity is encapsulated in activity theory (AT). We describe how this theory and its graphic representations have evolved over time. From an AT perspective, all human behaviour, including learners' response to written CF and teachers' feedback practices, is governed by certain accepted rules and norms of behaviour as well as by the individual participants' goals and beliefs.

In a nutshell, this chapter shows that SCT and its derivative AT attempt to provide an explanation for why written CF may or may not lead to L2 development in the case of a particular learner or a specific group of learners. Language development or lack thereof may be due to the nature of the feedback provided and its delivery. For feedback to be effective it needs to respond dynamically to an individual learner's potential rather than just existing language capacities (scaffolding and ZPD). The effectiveness of the feedback may also be shaped by how that feedback is delivered and processed (mediation and tools), as well as context and individual specific dimensions (activity theory). SCT and AT analyse these individual and contextual dimensions simultaneously (e.g. individual goals, relationships between participants), and as such provide an alternative explanation as to why written CF may or may not lead to L2 development.

1.3.4   Chapter 5

In this chapter, we critically review the body of research on written CF that has been informed by sociocultural theory (SCT) and activity theory (AT). This is a relatively modest body of research, and the studies are predominantly longitudinal case studies. We discuss the studies in terms of the key constructs outlined in the previous chapter. We begin by discussing studies which investigated the impact of scaffolded feedback provided by experts (teachers, researches) on learners' L2 development. Most of this research has included oral CF (in conferences) on students' writing rather than just written CF. We then discuss studies that have investigated the scaffolding strategies that peers employ in peer response activities and their impact on revision. We note that most of these studies have been descriptive rather than providing evidence on whether scaffolded teacher- or peer-provided-feedback leads to L2 development as measured by new writing.

When considering the role of mediation and tools in the provision of written CF, we review studies that investigated how language, a symbolic tool, mediates the processing of written CF. These studies rely predominantly on recorded pair talk, where learners deliberate on the written CF they received on their joint writing. The findings of these studies suggest that deliberations about the feedback (languaging) may improve the learners' ability to incorporate the feedback in revised drafts. We then review studies that investigated how the use of material tools, namely computer-mediated written CF, may impact on the quality of the feedback and learners' engagement with the feedback. In the majority of these studies, the focus is on peer feedback. We note again that this body of research lacks data concerning language development as evidenced in new writing.

In the final section, we review studies that employed AT in analysing the actions of feedback receivers (learners) and feedback providers (teachers and peers), taking into consideration the personal, interpersonal and institutional dimensions in a particular language-learning context. Unlike studies that adopt a cognitive perspective and consider context or learner dimensions (see Chapter 3), studies informed by AT attempt to consider all these dimensions simultaneously. These studies tend to employ a case study design and provide thick descriptions of the learners' behaviour (engagement with written CF) and of the context in which the activity takes place. In this way, they highlight the complexity of the feedback activity and thus help explain some of the mixed findings from research on the effects of written CF on L2 development.

1.3.5   Chapter 6

The final chapter summarises how cognitive and sociocultural perspectives view the role of written CF in L2 learning processes and why such feedback may or may not result in successful L2 development. We also reflect on the currently available research evidence on the contribution of written CF to L2 development, highlighting some of the gaps in the research informed by these two theoretical perspectives and identify future theoretical and research directions that could add to our knowledge in the field as L2 theorists, researchers and instructors. We conclude the chapter with a consideration of how the two perspectives can be seen as complementing one another in pedagogical practice.

2 The Cognitive Perspective on Written CF for L2 Development

2.0 Introduction

Since the early 1980s, our understanding of what constitutes and facilitates second language learning has been largely informed by theories and hypotheses about the cognitive processing of explicit L2 information. Drawing on the work of Piaget (1974), in the field of developmental psychology, which posited that 'multiple internal-cognitive and external-environmental factors interact reciprocally, and together contribute to the observed processes and outcomes of L2 learning' (Ortega, 2009: 55), SLA theorists focused their attention on understanding these processes and outcomes primarily as two separate activities until the mid-1990s. In this chapter, we focus our attention on what SLA theories and hypotheses have to say about cognitive information processing and the potential of written CF to facilitate such processing for L2 development. Towards the end of the chapter, we outline some of the individual internal and individual external factors that have more recently been hypothesised to facilitate or impede progress as learners reach a new stage in the cognitive process.

Theoretical accounts of L2 learning via cognitive processing have sought to explain (1) the nature of L2 knowledge and (2) the cognitive processes involved in its development. These accounts have largely been explained in terms of learning that occurs when learners communicate orally with native and non-native speakers of the target language because spontaneous oral language has been considered a better approximation of target-like competence. As a result, writing has tended to be seen as the result of acquisition rather than as a facilitating factor and as the most distant reflection of the learner's developing L2. However, in more recent years, questions have been asked about (1) what role writing and written CF can play in the learning process and (2) whether learning processes that occur in an oral context might also occur in a written context and (3) whether the written modality can provide any advantages that the oral modality is unable, or less able, to offer.

A growing number of researchers (Bitchener, 2012; Polio, 2012; Sheen, 2010; Williams, 2012) have commented on what might be argued as crucial advantages afforded by opportunities to write (as opposed to opportunities to speak), especially if learners receive written CF on the linguistic accuracy of their written output. The first advantage concerns the permanence of the written text. Learners can refer back to written texts as often as they wish but, when interacting orally, the spoken utterance is fleeting and is therefore unable to be revisited in the same way that a written statement can be. The second advantage afforded by writing opportunities is the additional time that learners have to think about what and how they write. The particular benefits of these affordances will be returned to at various places in this chapter.

Our aim in this chapter, then, is to explore (1) what SLA theories and hypotheses say about the cognitive processing of L2 information and hypothesise the extent to which written CF can play a role in this process and (2) the individual internal and external factors that may mediate the progress a learner makes in developing his or her L2 knowledge. Thus, we present a theoretical case or argument that supports a role for written CF in developing a learner's L2 knowledge. In doing so, we also acknowledge where some prominent counter-arguments have been proposed. We divide our case into the following sections:

- A consideration of the goal of L2 learning and its relationship to two types of linguistic competence (acquired and learnt) and of two types of knowledge (explicit and implicit) that have been identified in the SLA literature (Section 2.1)
- An account of the relationship between explicit and implicit knowledge, focusing on skill acquisition theories and the conversion of explicit knowledge to implicit knowledge (Section 2.2)
- The nature of input available to learners (Section 2.3)
- Stages in the cognitive processing of input (including written CF) for the development of explicit and implicit knowledge (Section 2.4)
- The consolidation of new knowledge and use over time (Section 2.5)
- The potentially mediating influences of individual and contextual factors on cognitive processing (Section 2.6)
- A summary of the case/argument we have presented in the chapter (Section 2.7)

2.1   The Relationship Between the Central Goal of L2 Learning and Two Types of Linguistic Competence and Knowledge

It is generally agreed that (1) the goal of L2 learning is the acquisition of native or near-native speaker competence in both understanding and producing/using the target language and that (2) this level of competence is most likely achieved when the learner can make a consistent, automatised, accurate and appropriate use of the target language under online conditions in oral communicative contexts (Ellis, 2009; Ortega, 2009). Krashen (1985) referred to this level of competence as **acquired competence** and distinguished it from **learnt competence** – that is, the type of competence that learners can achieve by paying conscious attention to the target language and its 'rules'. In terms of the linguistic knowledge that characterises these levels of competence, two types have been identified. Acquired competence draws on **implicit knowledge** while learnt competence makes use of **explicit knowledge** (Ellis, 2009). Implicit knowledge is the type that can be used automatically and without conscious attention. Explicit knowledge, on the other hand, involves the learner in a controlled, conscious consideration of what constitutes target-like accuracy and appropriateness, and is the type of knowledge that L2 learners are typically exposed to in educational/instructional contexts.

The existence of these two types of knowledge and competence has not been uncontroversial. In claiming that the two types of knowledge are located in separate parts of the brain, Krashen (1985, 1994, 2003), on the one hand, advanced the view that **learnt knowledge** cannot be converted to **acquired knowledge**. In the SLA literature, this is referred to as the non-interface position. Truscott (2004, 2007) also supports this position on the grounds that drawing upon explicit knowledge will, at best, only have a superficial effect, and will not facilitate L2 development over time. On the other hand, a growing number of interaction theorists argue that explicit knowledge can be converted to implicit knowledge. The **strong interface position** (DeKeyser, 1998) claims that explicit knowledge can be converted to implicit knowledge as a result of **practice** that is appropriately contextualised. The **weak interface position** (N. Ellis, 2005), while also stating that explicit knowledge can be converted to implicit knowledge, explains the limitations on how and when the conversion can occur. For instance, he argues that explicit knowledge of variational features (like the copula 'be') may be converted to implicit knowledge as a result of a memorisation of the form over time and, consequently, be used without conscious attention. On the other hand, he argues that explicit knowledge of developmental features (like negation) would only be expected to be converted if the learner was at the developmental stage required for using them without conscious attention.

A common claim in all these positions is that which sees explicit knowledge helping learners produce more accurate output if they are able to draw on their explicit knowledge during production. In addition, we would argue that an even stronger case might be made for drawing upon explicit knowledge from written CF because of the additional time that learners have for processing and using it when writing compared with the more limited time they have available when producing oral responses in normal conversational exchanges. On these grounds, then, it would seem reasonable to hypothesise that written CF has the potential to facilitate the development of explicit L2 knowledge and, through practice, the acquisition of implicit knowledge.

If this is the case, the key question one then needs to consider is how the conversion might occur. To answer this, we turn to explanations that have been provided in the skill acquisition theories of Anderson and McLaughlin.

2.2   Skill Acquisition Theories and the Conversion of Explicit Knowledge to Implicit Knowledge

Skill acquisition theories, in relation to language learning, are based on the view that language learning, like the learning of others skills, is characterised by the progression from an initial stage of **declarative knowledge** or knowledge about the skill (during which the learner is involved in conscious, controlled processing and practice) to a final **procedural stage** in which knowledge is automatically and unconsciously drawn upon.

2.2.1   Anderson's model

In Anderson's Adaptive Control of Thought Model (Anderson, 1976, 1980, 1983, 1993), a distinction is made between declarative knowledge and procedural knowledge. Although broadly speaking, the distinction aligns with the explicit-implicit distinction referred to in Section 2.0 above (Ellis, 2008), it should be acknowledged that they are actually neurobiologically different constructs: explicit knowledge must be declarative but implicit knowledge can be declarative or procedural (Paradis, 1994; Ullman, 2001). The model illustrates how progression from declarative to procedural knowledge takes place in three stages – **declarative, associative and autonomous** – and how **practice** is the key to progress from one stage to the next. As the following explanation (Mitchell and Myles, 2004) of the use of the third person –s illustrates, the **declarative stage** (in which a description of the procedure is learnt) shows that an –s must be added to the verb after the third person subject. The **associative stage** (in which a method for performing the skill is worked out) shows how to add an –s when the context requires it. It is during this stage that errors are most likely to occur. The **autonomous stage** (in which the skill becomes more and more rapid and automatic) shows that the learner adds an –s more and more automatically and unconsciously.

> If we take the example of the third person singular –s marker on present tense verbs in English, the classroom learner might initially know, in the sense that they have consciously learnt the rule, that s/he + verb requires the addition of an –s to the stem of the verb. However, the same learner might not necessarily be able to consistently produce the –s in a conversation in real time. This is because this particular learner has declarative knowledge of that rule, but it has not yet been proceduralized. After much practice, this knowledge will hopefully

become fully proceduralized, and the third person –s will be supplied when the conversation requires it. (Mitchell & Myles, 2004: 103)

Because **practice** is seen as the mechanism that facilitates progress from one stage to the next, it is important to have a clear understanding of what is meant by the term as it is intended in this context. Traditionally, practice has been viewed in L2 learning contexts as activity that involves the process of repeatedly and deliberately attempting to produce a specific feature of the target language, but, as DeKeyser (1998) explains, the importance of practice directed at behaviour rather than structures was missing from that focus. The mechanical practising of a linguistic feature in decontextualised activities (e.g. mechanical drills typical of behaviourist practice) was seen as unlikely to affect the learner's long-term memory and lead to a change of behaviour (i.e. from declarative processing to automatic processing). Thus, practice of the actual behaviour itself (i.e. attempts to communicate) is needed:

> Proceduralization is achieved by engaging in the target behaviour – or procedure – while temporarily leaning on declarative crutches ... Repeated behaviours of this kind allow the restructuring of declarative knowledge in ways that make it easier to proceduralize and allow the combination of co-occurring elements into larger chunks that reduce the working memory load. (DeKeyser, 1998: 49)

The importance of contextual practice can be further underscored by Transfer-Appropriate Processing (TAP) theory, which claims that information is best retrieved when the condition for retrieval matches the condition in which it is retrieved (Lightbown, 2006; Segalowitz & Lightbown, 1999).

2.2.2   McLaughlin's information processing model

Adding to our understanding of the specific cognitive processes and conditions involved in progressing from one stage to the next is McLaughlin's Information Processing Model. Drawing on insights about information processing from cognitive psychology, McLaughlin (1978, 1980, 1987, 1990), McLaughlin et al. (1983) and McLaughlin and Heredia (1996) posit the view that learners are limited in how much information they are able to consciously process at any one time because of (1) the nature and complexity of the oral or written task/activity they are performing and (2) their own information processing capacity. McLaughlin explains that, if learners are not capable of attending to all the information that is available in their long-term memory, they may need to selectively attend to certain aspects of it and only attend peripherally to other aspects of it.

In the Information Processing model, McLaughlin explains how learners first resort to **controlled processing** of explicit/declarative L2 information.

At this stage, a lot of attentional control is required, and there are likely to be limitations with the amount of information the learner can process in his/her working memory. McLaughlin adds that through repeated activation (that is, practice), sequences first produced by controlled processing can become **automatic**. He explains how these automatised sequences (i.e. implicit-procedural knowledge) are then stored as units in the **Long-Term Memory** and are made available very rapidly whenever the situation requires them, with minimal attentional control by the learner. It is important to note that the long-term memory stores explicit-declarative knowledge as well as implicit, proceduralised knowledge, and that this is accessed by learners when they compare their existing knowledge with new information, for example, when they compare written CF with their own written output. McLaughlin further explains that, as a result, automatic processes can work in parallel, activating clusters of complex cognitive skills simultaneously. When this shift occurs, controlled processes are freed to deal with higher levels of processing (i.e. to the integration of more complex skill clusters). This explains, then, the incremental nature of learning and development during which there is a progression from explicit, declarative knowledge to implicit, procedural knowledge and a constant restructuring of the learner's linguistic system as controlled processing gives way to more automatised responses.

2.2.3   Empirical evidence of the interface position

Therefore, to know if explicit knowledge can be developed through the conscious, controlled processing of L2 information, as these skill acquisition models suggest, empirical evidence is needed to validate the claims. One study that attempted to test the interface position was DeKeyser's (1997) investigation into the effects of two kinds of form-focused instruction (explicit-deductive and implicit-inductive) on two kinds of rules ('simple categorical rules' and 'fuzzy prototypical rules') in an artificial grammar called Autopractan. This grammar included 16 nouns and 16 verbs and had morphological markings for gender, number and case as well as flexible word order. The study comprised three stages: (1) the provision of explicit, declarative knowledge by means of picture-and-sentence exercises over six sessions; (2) practice in order to promote proceduralisation (i.e. the conversion from controlled to automatic performance); (3) testing the learners on four of the rules, using comprehension items (matching sentences read on a computer with one of four pictures) and production items (typing the sentence that best described a given picture). At stage two, negative feedback on the answers the learners gave during practice included explicit information of the error as well as the correct response. To understand the learning process, DeKeyser plotted the learners' reaction times and accuracy over the testing events at the end of each practice session and found (1) that responses became faster and more accurate over the first two sessions, (2) that they had stabilised by the fourth or fifth practice session and (3) that the speed and accuracy of the responses remained constant from that point onwards. As well as investigating the process of learning, the data from the post-tests conducted in the final session were examined to assess the learning outcomes. Gains were found to be skill-specific. From the findings, DeKeyser argued that learners who are taught explicit knowledge about linguistic form and then practice it are able to use it in a progressively more proceduralised manner.

Further evidence of the interface position has been reported in (1) Spada and Tomita's (2010) meta-analysis where explicit instruction led to the acquisition of implicit knowledge when operationalised as knowledge used in oral production and (2) oral feedback studies (Ellis *et al.*, 2006; Li, 2014) where metalinguistic feedback (supposedly leading to explicit knowledge) led to gains in tests of implicit knowledge (e.g. imitation). In order to understand the form this information processing can take, we need to consider first the nature of the input that learners are given to process.

2.3 Two Types of Input: Positive Evidence and Negative Evidence (Including Written CF)

Accounts of the cognitive processing and internalisation of explicit, declarative knowledge begin with the external provision of **input** from the environment. Two types of knowledge **input** can be made available to L2 learners: input comprising **positive evidence** (about what is linguistically acceptable in the target language in terms of well-formed linguistic form and structure) and input comprising **negative evidence, including CF** (about what is not acceptable in the target language).

In his Input Hypothesis, Krashen (1985) claimed that comprehensible input (positive evidence) alone is sufficient for L2 learning, but interactionists like Long (1996), Schmidt (1990, 1994, 2001), Swain (1985, 1995) and others argue (1) that exposure to positive L2 input alone is not sufficient for L2 learning and (2) that learners need to know when their output does not conform to L2 form/structure and be 'pushed' to modify it when negative feedback/CF indicates that there has been a problem (for example, a linguistic error has been made). In supporting their case, interactionists explain how research in content-based and immersion contexts, where levels of grammatical accuracy are often a lot lower than levels of L2 fluency, found that the availability of negative evidence/CF enabled learners to raise their level of accuracy (Swain, 1985; Swain & Lapkin, 1998).

If negative evidence in the form of oral CF can facilitate learning, as an increasing number of studies have reported (see overview of oral CF studies in Goo & Mackey, 2013; Loewen, 2011; Lyster & Ranta, 2013; Lyster, Saito & Sato, 2013), we need to ask whether or not it can also be expected to facilitate L2 development when provided as written CF. Because written CF, like oral CF, can be delivered in a variety of ways, it is important to understand what the different types are, how they differ from one another in terms of explicitness and whether any of them are more facilitative of L2 development than others.

2.3.1   Types of written CF as input

Three main types of written CF have been identified in the literature: direct CF, indirect CF and metalinguistic CF (Ellis, 2009). **Direct written CF** has typically been defined as that which provides some form of explicit correction of linguistic form or structure above or near the linguistic error. It may involve the crossing out of an unnecessary word, phrase or morpheme, the insertion of a missing word, phrase or morpheme, or the provision of the correct form or structure. **Indirect written CF** has been defined as that which indicates that an error has been made but it does not provide a correction. It may take the form of underlining or circling an error, thereby indicating and locating the error, or recording in the margin the number of errors in a given line, thereby indicating only that an error has been made somewhere in the line of text. **Metalinguistic CF** has been defined as that which provides the learner with an explanation of what has caused the error (and often this is in the form of grammar rules) and an example or examples of correct usage. This is usually done by giving each error a number and at the bottom of the page of text or at the end of the full text providing the metalinguistic explanation and example(s) beside the relevant number assigned to the error category in the learner's text. Metalinguistic information can also be provided in the form of a clue and usually an error code (e.g. art = article; prep = preposition) is used for this purpose.

Because each of these types of CF is provided in written form, they are, by definition, explicit forms of input and able to be used to develop the learner's explicit L2 knowledge. However, some types (e.g. metalinguistic CF) are more explicit than others because they supply more linguistic data than others (e.g. indirect underlining or errors) about (1) the cause of an error and (2) how to correct an error. This raises the question, then, about whether or not the more explicit types are better for L2 learning – a question that has been prominent in the empirical research (see Chapter 3) but less prominent in the theoretical literature.

2.3.2   Theoretical proposals on the effectiveness of different written CF types

Theoretically, explanations about why a particular type of written CF might be more effective than another type have been published over the years but they tend to be somewhat piecemeal and theoretically under-developed.

Those supporting **indirect** feedback have suggested that this approach is most useful because it invites the learner to 'engage in guided learning and problem-solving' (Lalande, 1982). In other words, learners need to do the work.

Typically, those more in favour of **direct** error correction suggest that it (1) reduces the type of confusion that learners may experience if they fail to understand indirect forms (namely, those just referred to), (2) provides them with information to help them resolve more complex errors (for example, more complex forms/structures and idiomatic usage), (3) offers more explicit feedback on hypotheses that may have been tested and (4) is more immediate. While these are certainly benefits of direct error correction, they may not be as helpful for learners who have partially acquired a particular form/structure and really need more explanation and practice in hypothesising and producing the correct form/structure themselves so that they can consolidate their knowledge and access it more automatically over time.

Explanations about the value of providing learners with **metalinguistic explanation** (written and/or oral) have not featured to a large extent in the earlier literature. Error codes, as a metalinguistic clue about why an error has occurred and therefore about how it might be corrected, have been mentioned but the potentially more informative information that can be provided in metalinguistic explanations (especially those that provide examples as well as rules and explanations) has not been discussed to any extent. Intuitively, one might expect metalinguistic explanation to be beneficial for learners at any level of proficiency insofar as it can (1) provide a form of initial instruction for new knowledge or (2) raise a learner's consciousness about what has been partially acquired. However, providing this most explicit type of feedback might not benefit more advanced learners' on-going L2 development/consolidation in the same way that indirect feedback may because the latter requires learners to determine what is incorrect with their production, hypothesise what a correct version would be as they draw upon their long-term memory store and process it in their working memory.

It may be that some of these types of CF are more effective than others at certain stages in the controlled processing of new L2 knowledge. We will examine these possibilities as we proceed with our overview of the key processing stages of a single feedback episode, described in the Gass (1997) framework.

2.4   Stages in the Cognitive Processing of Input/CF for the Development of Explicit and Implicit Knowledge

In framing our discussion of the processing of information in a single written CF episode, we draw upon the computational framework developed by Gass (1997) because (1) it brings together clearly and effectively the various hypotheses and constructs that explain the processing of explicit input/CF and (2), as Ellis (2008) explains, 'the model ... constitutes the fullest and clearest statement of the roles played by input and interaction in L2 acquisition currently available' (2008: 268). This computational framework describes five key stages in the cognitive processing of input and CF to modified output and new output: (1) attention to and noticing (apperception) of input, (2) comprehended input, (3) intake, (4) integration and (5) output. These five stages represent what has been described as a single written CF episode and are the first manifestation of learning from input/CF. The framework explains how additional episodes can be initiated if the learner fails to accurately modify his/her output. Figure 2.1, drawing upon the Gass (1997) framework, illustrates each of these stages in the processing of a single written CF episode. We consider each of these stages in turn.

2.4.1   Attention and noticing (apperception) of input/CF (Stage 1)

In order to benefit from CF as input when a linguistic error has been made, Gass (1997) explains that the learner needs to first apperceive or notice that there is a gap in his or her L2 knowledge. For this to occur, interactionists (Schmidt, 1990, 1994; Sharwood-Smith, 1981, 1993; Swain, 1985, 1995) argue that the learner needs to consciously **attend** to the input that has been provided. As Schmidt (1990, 1994, 2001) explains, with reference to the work of Tomlin and Villa (1994), there are three different levels of attention. The lowest level of attention is **alertness,** that is, the learner's motivation and readiness to learn. Motivation and readiness are very much individual factors, so they have the potential to play a significant role in whether learners choose to attend to CF. (nb. The role of these and other individual difference factors are discussed in detail in Section 2.6 of this chapter.)

The next level of attention, **orientation**, refers to the need for the learner's attention to be orientated towards a focus on form or linguistic accuracy, and not only to a focus on meaning. Thus, orientation 'entails the aligning of attention on some specific type or class of sensory information at the expense of others' (Ellis, 2008: 437). **Detection** is the highest level of attention, and this refers to the cognitive registration of a stimuli (e.g. CF) being present for the processing of information. It would seem, given the explicit nature of written CF, that a learner would have no difficulty **detecting** that some aspect of information about the L2 is being offered. Compared with the ambiguity that can sometimes arise in the oral context about whether or not recasts as CF are, in fact, CF and not just alternative forms of utterance (Lyster, 1998), the explicitness of written CF means that the learner is likely to realise its intent as CF, especially if it is one of the more explicit forms described above.

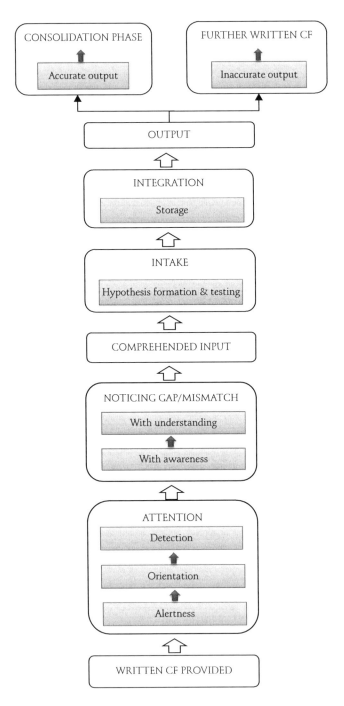

Figure 2.1 Stages in the cognitive processing of input/CF

At this point in the learner's cognitive readiness, Schmidt (1995) explains that the learner is ready to (1) **notice or apperceive** that some aspect of new linguistic information (be it positive or negative evidence) has been provided and, if the new information is in the form of CF, (2) **notice that there is a mismatch or gap** between his or her output and the target language input that has been provided in the CF response. He adds that '**noticing-with-awareness**' (at the point of encounter) that new information has been provided and that '**noticing-with-understanding**' are necessary to some extent for the effective processing of new L2 information. In the strong version of the Noticing Hypothesis, Schmidt (2001) argues that learners only learn what they **consciously attend** to in the input/CF they receive. By comparison, in the weak version of the hypothesis, he claims that individuals learn about the things they attend to and do not learn much about the things they do not attend to (Schmidt, 2001). **Noticing-with-awareness-and-with-understanding** would seem to be enhanced in the written context given the permanence and time available for this cognitive process. The fleeting nature of oral CF might give the learner less opportunity to notice-with-understanding but in the written context, the potential exists for the learner to consciously attend to the written CF over a longer period of time to make sure he/she understands what the written CF is saying.

Interactionists also explain how a range of **learner-internal** and **learner-external** factors can play a role in determining whether or not, and the extent to which, individual learners are likely to attend to and notice input/CF. Referring to the potential effect of such factors, Schmidt (2001) writes:

> The allocation of attention is the pivotal point at which learner-internal factors (including aptitude, motivation, current L2 knowledge, and processing ability) and learner-external factors (including the complexity and the distributional characteristics of input, discoursal and interactional context, instructional treatment, and task characteristics) come together. What then happens within attentional space largely determines the course of language development, including the growth of knowledge (the establishment of new representations), fluency (access to that knowledge), and variation. (Schmidt, 2001: 39)

Limited consideration has been given in the theoretical literature to how individual learner-internal factors (both cognitive and motivational/affective) might impact on attention and noticing as well as on other stages of cognitive processing described below. Although we discuss the potential effect of these factors in a separate section below (Section 2.6) and in Chapter 4, we continue to signal where they might play a moderating role in this overview of the five cognitive processing stages of the computational model.

2.4.2   ComprehendED input (Stage 2)

The second stage of the Gass (1997) framework picks up on Schmidt's noticing-with-understanding and shows that input/CF needs to be **comprehendED** before it can become **intake** (stage three). Comprehended input, as Gass explains, is not the same as comprehensible input (Long, 1981, 1996); whereas the latter positions the speaker as the one controlling comprehensibility, the former refers to whether or not the learner has actually comprehended the input/CF. When the learner is provided with written CF, the extent to which it is comprehended may depend on how explicit the feedback is, and therefore on the type of CF provided. For example, highly explicit metalinguistic information with grammatical explanations and examples may help the learner comprehend more clearly and fully than less explicit types like the underlining or circling of errors, especially, if the learner has only partially stored in his/her long-term memory information about when and why the particular linguistic form or structure is required. Thus, the L2 proficiency level of the learner as well as the nature and extent of the learner's stored knowledge in the long-term memory will likely determine if the CF is comprended. For less proficient learners and for those with limited partially acquired knowledge, more explicit types of written CF may be more helpful whereas less explicit types of feedback may be sufficient for more advanced learners who possess a larger store and who are likely to have had more retrieval experience. Although written CF that is not comprehended is unlikely to be internalised, Gass argues that the learner's comprehension may be gradual; it may begin with an understanding of the meaning and progress to an understanding of other components such as form and structure.

2.4.3   Intake (Stage 3)

The next stage of the processing framework requires the learner to match the input/CF he or she has received with his/her existing knowledge. As Gass (1997) reminds us, the learner's existing knowledge is not only knowledge of the L2 but may also include the native language knowledge and knowledge of other languages. She also notes that universal principles of language may play a role in the internalisation process (see Ellis, 2008, Chapter 12, for an overview of Universal Grammar). The matching process involves different levels of analysis and re-analysis in the **working memory** as comparisons are made between the learner's existing knowledge, retrieved from his/her **long-term memory**, and the input/CF that has been received. In the process of comparing both sets of knowledge, the learner can make hypotheses about what is acceptable and not acceptable in the L2. It may be that working memory (a construct for online simultaneous storage and for the processing of information) has a less significant role to play in writing tasks, including the processing of written CF, than it has in oral communication where the engagement period is fleeting and finite (Kormos, 2012; Williams, 2012).

As we indicated earlier, writing opportunities, as opposed to speaking opportunities, may provide learners with better conditions in which to match the input/written CF they receive with their existing L2 knowledge because of (1) the permanence of the text (enabling the learner to refer back to what he wrote and to what the feedback says as often as desired) and (2) the greater amount of time that the learner has, as a writer, for analysis and re-analysis.

Of all the individual difference factors that may mediate the learner's information processing, the **processing capacity** and **language learning aptitude** of the learner may play critical roles in the matching of new information with existing knowledge in the long-term memory. We discuss these possibilities in Sections 2.6.1.1 and 2.6.1.2 below.

2.4.4   Integration (Stage 4)

As each **hypothesis** is tested by means of a modification to the learner's original output, any one of four outcomes is possible in the process of **integration**. First, the learner's existing L2 hypothesis, drawn from knowledge stored in the long-term memory, will be either confirmed or rejected. Acceptance occurs when the input/CF is the same as the learner's existing hypothesis and it is rejected when the hypotheses are different. When the hypothesis is rejected, the learner has the opportunity to form another hypothesis and have this confirmed or rejected when further input/CF is provided. Any amount of restructuring or modification of the learner's new hypotheses can therefore occur. The second potential outcome of hypothesis-testing is a strengthening of the learner's current hypothesis through a confirmation of the accuracy of a new use of the linguistic item. Rightly or wrongly, the absence of written CF may signal to the learner that his/her output is accurate. However, it may be simply an oversight on the part of the provider or a more intentional 'let-it-pass' decision. The more often each hypothesis is confirmed, the more the learner's L2 knowledge is likely to be consolidated. The third possible outcome is storage. At this point, the information in the input is not immediately incorporated into the learner's L2 knowledge system but is stored until the learner has received more evidence about the acceptability of the hypothesis. Then, it is confirmed or rejected. The fourth possible outcome is one in which the hypothesis may exit from the processing system because the learner realises it is incorrect.

Hypothesis-testing in the written context would seem to be facilitated by the time that the learner has to retrieve existing knowledge from the long-term memory and to make cognitive comparisons between it and the written CF they have received. As Williams (2012) suggests, 'it is probably safe to say that the cognitive window is open somewhat wider and that learners have a richer opportunity to test their hypotheses when they write than when they speak' (2012: 328). One advantage of hypothesis-testing that results from processing written CF may be that learners feel more comfortable doing it in this modality than in more public settings where issues of face and identity may be more threatened if hypotheses prove to be incorrect. As Williams (2012) puts it, 'the written mode can be a lower stakes arena in which to test out emergent forms' (2012: 328).

2.4.5   Output (Stage 5)

Output, be it modified output or new output in response to CF, is the overt manifestation of whether or not the learner has begun the process of developing new explicit knowledge. If the modified output or new output does not reveal an accurate use of the L2, the learning process may need to return to the initial input/CF stage. On the other hand, it may be that the effect is delayed. Once a learner's hypothesis has been confirmed as an accurate use of the L2, the initial processing episode is completed. Even though the learner has successfully produced accurate output as a result of the cognitive processing that was triggered by the CF input he/she received, this is no guarantee that accurate output will always be produced on subsequent occasions when the form or structure is required.

There are a number of factors that might explain why a learner might fail on some occasions to produce accurate output while on other occasions be able to produce an accurate use of the form or structure. Each time the form or structure is required, the learner needs to be cognitively aware of the need to use it. In this regard, the role of the learner's working memory is crucial (as we explain in Section 2.6.1.1 below). The learner needs to have attentional control over the production of meaning and appropriate form/structure and be able to retrieve the newly integrated information from the long-term memory for processing it in the working memory. Additionally, a number of individual and contextual factors may play a mediating role in the cognitive processing of the learner's working memory and in the production of accurate output. These will also be discussed in Section 2.6 below. Having produced accurate output on one occasion, through the cognitive processing of a single episode described above, the learner then needs to consolidate this new knowledge over time with further practice in retrieving the stored knowledge and in accurately using the form/structure.

2.5   Beyond the Single Written CF Episode – Knowledge Consolidation

As skill acquisition theories explain, repeated retrievals of explicit, declarative knowledge from the learner's long-term memory during meaningful practice that is sustained over time have the potential to provide the learner with opportunities for deeper processing, less controlled processing and more rapid, automatised processing. Interface theorists claim that when the learner becomes less reliant on controlled retrieval and processing, future retrievals have the potential to become more automatic and the knowledge retrieved more implicit even though the explicit knowledge remains. When a learner is able to produce over time an accurate use of the L2 in oral contexts, where time and permanence are not characteristics of the processing conditions in this context, one would be more inclined to suggest that implicit knowledge has been developed. In the writing process, it is potentially more difficult to know if the learner has drawn upon implicit knowledge than it might be when output is produced in online oral conversation.

Now that we have scoped the key stages of a single CF processing episode and outlined the need for consolidation, it is important to consider the range of factors that might facilitate or impede the learner's cognitive processing of input/CF during both the controlled processing of information in the initial feedback episode and subsequent consolidation stages. Individual learners are not computers, so we need to consider at what stages a learner's cognitive processing might fail to proceed and whether certain individual internal and external factors may be likely causes. As Kormos (2012) explains, 'individual differences may be hypothesised to exert influence on how students process feedback, the extent to which they notice gaps in their knowledge, the aspects of language they pay attention to, and, consequently, how they exploit the learning opportunities provided by writing' (Kormos, 2012: 400).

2.6   The Potentially Mediating Influence of Individual and Contextual Factors on Cognitive Processing

Factors that may impact upon cognitive processing include individual learner-**internal cognitive** factors (working memory and processing capacity; language learning aptitude), individual learner-**internal**

motivational/affective factors (goals, interest, attitudes, beliefs) and individual learner-**external** factors (macro and micro contexts, pedagogical and instructional factors, social relationships). In the wider SLA literature, the effect of these factors on language learning processes and outcomes has been found to differ from individual to individual (Ellis, 2008). Compared with earlier understandings of their individual effects, recent SLA research has found these factors to be both inter-related and dynamically interacting (Dornyei, 2010). In terms of the effect they might have on the cognitive processing of written CF, only limited speculation has been offered in the literature, and even less empirical testing of hypothetical possibilities has been reported. Thus, it is important that consideration be given to what these possibilities might be.

We divide this discussion into three sections: (1) individual learner-internal cognitive factors (Section 2.6.1), (2) individual learner-internal motivational/affective factors (Section 2.6.2) and (3) individual learner-external factors (Section 2.6.3). In each section, we define the factors and consider where and how they might facilitate or impede the learner's cognitive processing of written CF, both within a single written CF episode and when practising and consolidating subsequent uses of their knowledge.

2.6.1   Individual learner-internal cognitive factors

Whether or not the learner attends to the written CF provided and, if s/he does so, the extent to which attention to it is sustained may be dependent upon (1) the learner's working memory (where the processing of input occurs) and processing capacity and (2) the learner's language learning aptitude.

2.6.1.1   The learner's working memory and processing capacity

The learner's working memory is the site where new input/CF is stored and integrated with information already encoded in the long-term memory and therefore where automatic and controlled cognitive processing occurs. Thus, it is here that key processes such as attention, noticing, hypothesising, restructuring and practice take place. Unlike the long-term memory, the working memory is of limited capacity and therefore constrained by the amount of information and processing it can work with at any one time. The capacity-limited model (e.g. Skehan, 1998) explains that the learner's working memory is limited in capacity and that learners with larger working memory capacities are better equipped to attend to and process input. In particular, the model proposes that lower proficiency learners may have difficulty attending to more than one aspect of language (e.g. form and meaning) simultaneously. On the other hand, the multiple-resources model (e.g. Robinson, 2003) suggests that there are separate resource pools (e.g. for auditory and visual processing), with competition for resources taking place within the working memory, but that competition does not take place between pools (e.g. attending to one aspect of language in the auditory medium and another in the visual medium).

Because learners with a lower level of proficiency need to process new information in a more consciously controlled manner, more effort and attention may need to be given in their working memory to noticing gaps in their linguistic knowledge, to the encoding of linguistic form and structure, and to testing new hypotheses about correct usage. Even if, as has been suggested earlier, the written context may be able to provide better opportunities for the processing of input/CF than the oral communication context, the learner's working memory still needs to coordinate the attention that learners give to cognitive processing, especially if they are attending to input over a longer period of time (e.g. if they analyse and reanalyse the input with their existing knowledge in their long-term memory). On each new occasion, during the consolidation phase, after written CF has been provided and an accurate reformulation has been achieved, the learner's working memory will be the site where retrieval from the long-term memory and production occur. Over time, as the new information is proceduralised, it is proposed that less demand will be placed on the learner's working memory, attentional resources and processing capacity. In all stages of information processing and production, it is expected that individuals will differ, and that differences may relate to different working memory spans. In discussing the role of working memory in the processing of oral input, Robinson (2005) and others (e.g. Miyake & Friedman, 1998; Sawyer & Ranta, 2001) have suggested that there is a relationship between the learner's working memory capacity and learning aptitude. The extent to which the relationship may also exist when working memory processes written input/CF will now be considered in Section 2.6.1.2.

2.6.1.2   The learner's language learning aptitude

Aptitude has been described as a complex construct that is distinct from general intelligence and achievement (Ellis, 2008). Language learning aptitude, in particular, is a special ability for learning another language. According to Carroll (1981), a language learner's cognitive profile comprises four components and, as Ellis (2008) explains, components (3) and (4) are the most distinguishing of learners with high language learning aptitude: (1) phonetic coding ability (ability to identify distinct sounds, to form associations between those sounds and symbols representing them, and to retain these associations); (2) grammatical sensitivity (ability to recognise the grammatical functions of words or other linguistic entities in sentence structures); (3) rote learning ability (the ability to learn associations between sounds and meanings rapidly and efficiently, and to retain these associations) and (4) inductive learning ability (the ability to infer or induce the rules governing a set of language materials, given sample language materials that permit such inferences).

So what role might language learning aptitude play at different stages of the cognitive processing of new knowledge? If learners have high language analytic ability, that is, an ability to combine high levels of grammatical sensitivity with effective inductive ability , they may be more likely to (1) notice the grammatical difference or gap between their output and new CF input, (2) make connections between the new input and their existing knowledge in the long-term memory, (3) process the CF input more deeply, or as Schmidt (2001) puts it, notice with awareness-as-understanding and (4) engage in problem-solving activity when they are aware in subsequent writing tasks during the consolidation phase that a gap exists in their knowledge or they are momentarily uncertain of the correct form or structure to use. Additionally, different types of CF (oral and written) might benefit analytically strong learners to a greater extent than analytically weak learners. For example, the former might find it easier to make use of metalinguistic CF and compare it with their existing knowledge. If learners make effective use of metalinguistic feedback in this way, it would seem likely that they would be able to process it more deeply.

2.6.2   Individual learner-internal motivational and affective factors

In addition to the effect that these individual learner-internal cognitive factors might have on the learner's attention, noticing and processing of input/CF, there are other individual learner-internal factors, such as those with a motivational and affective component, that may also moderate a learner's attention and processing. Despite the amount of theorising and research that has been published in the SLA literature about language learning motivation, little attention has been given to the way L2 learners respond to, attend to and process written CF as new knowledge. We begin this section with an overview of the key constructs in motivation research and speculate on their potential to affect the learner's attention to and processing of written CF: goals and interest in Section 2.6.2.1 and attitudes and beliefs in Section 2.6.2.2.

2.6.2.1   *Goals and interest*

As Dornyei (2001) and Dornyei and Ushioda (2009) explain, motivation explains why people **select** a particular activity, how long they are willing to **persist** at it, and what effort they are willing to **invest** in it. Selection is often associated with an individual's **goals** (Gardner, 1985, 2006), be they (1) instrumental goals (associated with the utilitarian value of learning another language), (2) integrative goals (associated with a learner's desire to become a part of the target language community) or (3) international posture goals (associated with an individual's 'interest in foreign or international affairs, willingness to go overseas to study or work, readiness to interact with intercultural partners ... and a non-ethnocentric attitude toward different cultures' (Yashima, 2002: 57).

To what extent, then, can these goals have an effect on language learning and its processes? Deci and Ryan (1985) explain in their distinction between **intrinsic** and **extrinsic** motivation that language learning goals such as these may only have a motivational influence if they are sufficiently internalised. If a learner is intrinsically motivated to learn a new language, it is because he/she finds the language and the learning of it interesting and enjoyable (Noels *et al.*, 2001). On the other hand, if a learner is extrinsically motivated, language learning may be undertaken to gain some kind of reward or advantage. Learners who have well established goals and a high level of interest in learning a particular target language might be expected to manifest a higher level of motivation throughout the attentional and processing stages than learners with less established goals and a lower level of interest. As a result, the former might be likely to (1) exhibit all three levels of attention identified by Tomlin and Villa (1994), (2) make every effort to notice and repair knowledge gaps in their L2 knowledge when input such as written CF makes this known, (3) persevere with hypothesis-testing on what constitutes correct usage of form and structure and (4) sustain this effort over time as new knowledge is consolidated and proceduralised. Even though this type of motivation would typically be expected of a learner with clear and established language learning goals and a high level of interest in learning the target language, it might also be moderated by other intervening factors that interrupt this level of effort and perseverance from time to time. Such factors might include any number of the learner-external factors (e.g. social, contextual, pedagogical) discussed below in Section 2.6.3.

2.6.2.2 *Attitudes and beliefs*

Attitudes to language learning in general, to target language communities, to the learning of a particular target language, to a focus on form and/or meaning, to written CF and particular types of written CF have also been identified in the SLA literature as motivational factors. As such, they can operate on an emotional level and influence whether a learner initiates language learning processes. For example, in relation to written CF, they might affect whether or not learners are ready and willing to attend to written accuracy, and therefore to written CF, and engage in cognitive processing activities such as comparison-making and hypothesis-testing. Also, if learners are given a particular type of written CF and do not believe it is helpful, they may decide to ignore it, that is, not attend to it and not cognitively process it. Such a situation could arise, for example, if prior experiences in being given that type of written CF did not enable them to accurately modify linguistic errors. Such experiences, together with their wider self-efficacy beliefs (i.e. a capacity to carry out a particular learning activity) may be factors in their de-motivation (Bandura, 1997; Pajares, 2003).

Motivated learning behaviour over time requires effort and persistence (Dornyei, 2001, 2005; Gardner, 1985, 2006) and is therefore necessary if learners are to become self-regulated in the sense that they can consciously organise and manage their learning behaviours (e.g. their competency beliefs, emotional thoughts, attitudes and responses while learning, their approaches to different language learning activities and different language learning contexts). Motivated learning behaviour would seem to be necessary if learners are to consolidate and proceduralise their new knowledge so that it can be retrieved automatically from their long-term memory over time.

2.6.3   Individual learner-external factors

Individual learner-external factors include a wide range of environmental and contextual factors that are further characterised by an equally wide range of social and pedagogical influences. Any one of these factors or influences has the potential to interact with the individual learner-internal factors identified above, especially those that can affect an individual learner's language learning motivation.

In this section, we identify some of the most prominent external factors to have been reported in the SLA literature with regard to L2 learning and speculate on the extent to which they might interact with individual motivational factors and together influence a learner's attention to and cognitive processing of written CF. We frame this discussion around the often-reported distinction between macro and micro contexts and setting.

2.6.3.1   Macro contexts and settings

Of the several types of macro setting that have been identified in the SLA literature, the two most germane to our discussion are second and foreign language learning settings. It has been argued (1) that the value of writing and of language learning from writing activities might vary according to these contexts and (2) that learners' experiences in these contexts might shape their writing goals, their attitudes to and beliefs about writing and their orientation to language learning through writing activities (Kormos, 2012). In particular, the latter includes the learners' orientation to focusing on form and therefore their response to and cognitive processing of written CF. Hedgecock and Lefkowitz (1994) have suggested that foreign language learners may be less motivated, less orientated to focusing on form, and therefore less likely to attend to written CF because their learning goal is more likely to be a qualification than an ability to use the target language accurately and appropriately as a member of the target language community. On the other hand, it could be argued that foreign language learners may be more focused on accuracy than second language learners because their instructional activities are typically more focused on grammatical accuracy than on communicating meaning in everyday situations. Even if one of these patterns is characteristic of a particular setting, it is also possible that individual learners may have goals, attitudes and processing orientations that depart from those of the majority. Whatever the individual goals and attitudes of the learner are, it is likely also that they will play a role in developing their self-efficacy beliefs and in fostering either an interest or disinterest in language learning and linguistic accuracy.

We can see, then, that within a single context there may be a complex interaction between external and internal motivational factors, and that these may determine whether or not a learner is likely to respond positively to written CF by attending to it. Not only can it be speculated that these factors may play an important role in preparing the learner to receive written CF, but it can also be predicted that they may continue to have an effect on the learner's on-going attention and processing beyond a single written CF episode during the consolidation process when new linguistic environments present the learner with the need to retrieve such knowledge for use in the writing of a new text.

2.6.3.2 Micro contexts and settings

There is some evidence to suggest that interest in and attitudes to language learning through writing and a focus on form can be triggered 'environmentally' (Hidi & Renninger, 2006) at the micro contextual level of the classroom. The nature of the social setting and the focus or priorities of an instructional programme may play a role in shaping a learner's beliefs about effective language learning practices, in fostering particular language learning goals and attitudes in developing an interest in the value of writing for language learning and in shaping a learner's self-efficacy beliefs and self-esteem.

Social setting factors such as those between teacher and learner and leaner and other learners have been shown in the SLA literature to play a role in the type of interaction that might or might not occur (Dornyei, 2005; Ellis, 2008). However, little consideration has been given to the effect that social relationships in the classroom might have on a learner's response to and processing of input/written CF. It may be that learners who have a positive attitude to their teacher and who respect their knowledge and interest in their learning activity are more responsive to the decisions that their teachers make. If this is the case, it may be that such learners will be more responsive to their teacher's decisions about when to give written CF and about what type or amount of feedback to give. Learners who have this type of relationship with their teacher may develop a stronger interest in the learning process and be more motivated than other learners to initiate and sustain the type of cognitive processing needed to develop a more automatised use of new linguistic knowledge. Learner-learner relationships have been shown in the SLA literature (see Ellis, 2008; Lightbown & Spada, 2011) to have an effect on the quality of oral interaction, and this is understandable given that some learners may or may not want to interact with other learners. This relationship may be less likely to have an effect on their response to writing activities and written CF, except perhaps when the tasks are collaboratively performed. In Chapter 4, we say more about the potential effect of social relationships in our discussion of the contribution of sociocultural perspectives to understanding L2 development.

Another micro contextual factor that might have an effect on a learner's response to written CF is the instructional focus of the language learning classroom. Different instructional practices may be characteristic of different types of classroom. For instance, in foreign language learning classrooms, a focus on form and written activities (both writing exercises and writing tasks) may be more common than in second language learning classrooms and immersion classrooms where a focus on effective oral communication may be given greater priority. In the former context, learners may be more likely to receive written CF on their writing than learners in the latter context. As a result, these experiences may have an influence on whether they develop an interest in receiving written CF and on their attitudes and beliefs about the value of writing activities and written CF. Thus, the level of exposure a learner has to writing tasks and written CF in current and former classroom contexts might determine the level of motivation they have for attending to and processing written CF (Bitchener & Ferris, 2012; Ferris, 1999; Reid, 1998, 2005; Roberts, 1999).

The type of writing task that learners are given in the classroom may also have an effect on their motivation to complete the task and use written CF. If learners are not motivated to do certain types/genres/topics of writing tasks, it may mean that they are not motivated to focus on the accuracy of their writing or to respond to any written CF that is given on the task. A learner may be unmotivated to engage with a writing task for a number of reasons: a lack of understanding about what the task requires, a lack of content knowledge that is required to complete the task, personal and situational circumstances that may be impacting on the learner at the time the task is given, a belief that doing the task has no value or interest for him/her as a learner, and so on. Any of these factors has the potential to draw the learner's attention away from the task of writing and of responding to written CF.

2.7   Summary

In this chapter, we set out to present a case that supports a role for written CF in L2 development, drawing upon theoretical perspectives that have something to say about the cognitive processing of L2 information and the potential of written CF as explicit L2 input to facilitate such processing. We began by explaining that the central goal of L2 learning is typically the acquisition of native or near-native speaker competence. In doing so, we argued that acquired competence which draws upon implicit knowledge can be developed from learnt competence which draws upon explicit knowledge such as that provided by written CF. Explaining this process, we referred to the skill acquisition theoretical models of Anderson and McLaughlin which show how explicit, declarative L2 knowledge can be proceduralised through meaningful, contextualised practice over time to a point where it is converted to implicit, acquired knowledge. We then described the specific information processing stages that have been identified by cognitive theorists (e.g. Tomlin & Villa, Schmidt, and Swain) and that have been represented in the framework designed by Gass (1997). In processing written CF as input, Gass' framework explains that learners need to attend to written CF as input if they are to progress through the other stages that will enable them to produce modified accurate output and on-going accurate output in new written texts over time. The other stages include an understanding (comprehendED input), an internalisation and an integration of written CF as input. Producing accurate output as a result of this conscious processing is the beginning of a longer consolidation process during which practice is believed to facilitate acquired competence. We acknowledged the possibility that this linear route towards acquisition may be both facilitated and interrupted as a result of the type of written CF a learner is provided with and as a result of intervening individual internal (cognitive and motivational/affective) factors and individual external factors. The extent to which these theoretical proposals are valid explanations of the contribution of written CF to L2 development is something that only empirical research can determine. The extent to which written CF research has focused on these proposals is the subject of Chapter 3.

3 Cognitively Informed Research on Written CF for L2 Development

3.0 Introduction

The aim of this chapter is to critically review the cognitively informed research on the contribution of written CF to L2 development. Although the focus of this research has tended to be more pedagogically motivated than theoretically motivated (Polio, 2012), it would be incorrect to assume that the absence of research questions explicitly focused on why written CF has the potential to facilitate L2 development signals that the research has not been theoretically informed. The theoretical case presented in Chapter 2 described both the cognitive processes involved and the product arising from the processing (that is, accurate output resulting from the provision of written CF input). In this chapter, it will be seen from the research that there has been more of a focus on the product arising from written CF than on the processing of explicit input. Thus, the focus is on (1) the extent to which written CF facilitates improved accuracy in text revisions and in the writing of new texts (that is, the product/output, immediately after written CF has been provided and in the writing of new texts over time) and (2) factors/variables that may facilitate or impede improved output. We also explain that, until recently, little attention has been given to (1) the cognitive processing of explicit information supplied by written CF (as discussed in Chapter 2) and (2) the extent to which individual and contextual factors may impact upon a learner's response to and cognitive processing of the input (also discussed in Chapter 2).

In the following sections of this chapter, we examine the key questions that have focused on the contribution of written CF to L2 development. The first, and arguably, the most important question is that which seeks to find out whether or not written CF has the potential to facilitate new L2 knowledge. We operationalise new knowledge as that which results in improved written accuracy and as that which may be a consolidation of partially acquired knowledge or a creation of completely new knowledge.

This question is both theoretically and pedagogically motivated. It is theoretical in terms of its focus on whether written CF, as one form of explicit negative evidence, can facilitate L2 development and pedagogical in terms of the extent to which the practice of providing learners with written CF on their written errors is able to produce modified and on-going accurate output. Thus, from a pedagogical perspective, it focuses on whether written CF, as explicit input 'works' and to what extent it 'works'. For instance, does it 'work' only immediately after it has been provided or over time as well?

The second research question is one that researchers and teachers have devoted a considerable amount of time to. It seeks to determine whether certain types of written CF are more effective for L2 development than others. This question has tended to be investigated from more of a pedagogical perspective in order to see if certain practices pay greater developmental dividends than others. Theoretically, it is also of interest and importance insofar as there are different views on whether more or less explicit types of written CF are more facilitative of L2 development. The extent to which different types may play a role in the information processing stages of development (see Chapter 2) has only very recently started to be a focus of written CF research.

Two other research questions that have been prominent in the literature, and which have been investigated from a more pedagogical perspective, include those that seek to find out (1) whether written CF is more effective when targeting certain linguistic domains and error categories (outlined in Chapter 2) and (2) whether a focused or targeted approach to the provision of written CF is more effective than an unfocused or more comprehensive approach (see Section 3.4). Our discussion of the findings of these investigations will explain why they should also be of theoretical interest.

Finally, questions focusing on whether or not, and the extent to which, individual and contextual factors may facilitate or impede L2 development have, to date, been more interested in exploring their effect on output (the product), both immediately and over time. Only a few recent studies have begun to examine their impact on the processing of written CF information. Studies with a processing focus will help us understand more fully *how* and *why* learners benefit, or fail to benefit, from the written CF they are provided with on particular occasions.

As we consider each of these questions, we draw attention to (1) shortcomings in the research and (2) further research that might enable the questions to be answered more fully. We end the chapter with a summary of key findings and draw some conclusions about their contribution to theory and pedagogy.

3.1   Can Written CF Facilitate L2 Development?

Since the publication of Truscott's (1996) paper, this question has tended to dominate research agendas. Prior to his call for the abandonment of written CF, researchers and practitioners had scarcely questioned whether it might *not* play a role in L2 learning. However, in response to the claims made by Truscott, researchers and teacher-researchers realised that the only way to find out whether or not his claims were valid was to produce empirical evidence in support of the practice or against it.

To answer the question in terms of the output or product arising from a response to written CF, pre-test/treatment (provision of written CF)/post-test designs have been employed, comparing accuracy performance before written CF is provided on linguistic errors (pre-test writing task) with performance immediately after receiving written CF (immediate post-test writing task – either pre-test revision or a new text or both) and at various periods of time thereafter (delayed post-tests). If learners in the groups that receive written CF reveal a significant increase in accuracy between their pre-test and immediate post-test scores and this increase is statistically higher than that of other learners (in a control group) who do not receive written CF, it is understood that written CF has, at least, begun to facilitate the learning process. If increases in accuracy are maintained in delayed post-tests, it is understood that learning is in the process of being consolidated.

To evaluate what the research has found about the contribution of written CF to L2 development, we review each of the studies. First, we consider, in Section 3.1.1 below, whether text revisions can predict L2 development and second, in Section 3.1.2 below, we examine the more extensive research that has focused on the writing of new texts over time.

3.1.1   Can text revisions contribute to L2 development?

Second language learners are often asked to revise their texts after they have been given written CF to see (1) if they have learnt anything from the feedback and (2) if they can then make accurate use of the learning in revising their texts. If an error is revised accurately, it is assumed that the learner has probably understood the feedback. Whether or not this constitutes L2 learning or development is, of course, unclear. It may signal that learning or development has been initiated, but unless the learner is given the opportunity to draw upon such knowledge when writing new texts over time, it is impossible to know whether the learning process has begun. This point was well made by Truscott (2007) when he wrote:

A writing task that students do with help from the teacher (the revision) is obviously not comparable to one they do on their own (the original essay) and so a study with this design does not yield any measure of learning, short-term or otherwise. (2007: 257)

The comment was made in response to several claims in articles on early written CF studies that learning had been demonstrated through the accurate revision of an original text. These studies are summarised in Table 3.1 below.

In order to demonstrate whether revised accuracy (such as that shown above) can be predictive of learning, two further studies (Truscott & Hsu, 2008; Van Beuningen *et al.*, 2008, 2012) investigated whether improved accuracy in a text revision was also evident in the writing of a new text. Truscott and Hsu (2008) reported that the accuracy improvement shown by their treatment group on the revision of a text was not evident when their learners wrote a new text. They concluded that written CF is not useful as a **learning** tool even though they acknowledged that it might have some limited, short-term value as an **editing** tool. Reflecting on this conclusion, Bruton (2009) questioned whether such a claim was valid because the learners had made very few errors in their first piece of writing, leaving little room for improvement.

Table 3.1 The effectiveness of written CF and text revisions

Studies	Participants	Treatment	Error categories	Effectiveness
Ashwell, 2000	50 EFL at a Japanese university	1. Content then form 2. Form then content 3. Form and content 4. Control (underlining or circling)	Grammatical Lexical Mechanical	yes
Fathman & Whalley, 1990	72 ESL at US colleges	1. Underlining 2. Control	Comprehensive	Yes
Ferris & Roberts, 2001	72 ESL at US colleges	1. Error code 2. Underlining 3. Control	Verb, noun ending, article errors, wrong word, sentence structure	Yes

On the other hand, the findings by Van Beuningen *et al.*, in both their pilot study (2008) of 62 learners and in their main study (2012) of 268 learners, contradict those reported by Truscott and Hsu (2008). In their pilot study, both treatment groups (direct error correction and error code) improved their accuracy in the text revision but only the first treatment group (direct error correction) revealed improved accuracy in the writing of a new text one week later. In the main study (2012), similar findings were reported for improved accuracy in the learners' text revisions but, in the writing of two new texts (four weeks apart), improved accuracy was demonstrated by both treatment groups. Given these different findings and the availability of so few studies on this issue, we believe it would be unwise to draw any conclusions at this stage. We believe that this is a question that needs more research because (1) text revision is a pedagogical practice employed by many classroom teachers and (2) it can be argued that any opportunity to hypothesise and produce output may be facilitative of the learning process.

Sometimes, however, L2 learners are not asked to revise an original text before writing a new text. They may be given some time in class to (1) look at the feedback and think about what they have received and (2) ask questions about it before doing a new piece of writing. This is most typically the practice that teachers adopt when written CF has not been in the form of direct error correction. The reason for this is clear; there is nothing for the learner to actually revise when a correction has been provided by the teacher. Most of the studies that have investigated the potential of written CF to facilitate L2 development have provided learners with a period of time (usually 5–10 minutes) to look over and think about the feedback they have been given before they write a new text.

3.1.2   Can improved accuracy in the writing of new texts over time contribute to L2 development?

As a result of Truscott's (1996) call for the abandonment of written CF, it is not surprising that much of the written CF research has, since then, focused on trying to answer this key question with regard to the evidence observed in the writing of new texts over time. Before considering this research (in Section 3.1.2.2), we review four early studies that were published before Truscott's (1996) paper (in Section 3.1.2.1) to indicate why their designs and execution were unable to provide convincing answers to the question.

3.1.2.1   The early studies (pre-Truscott, 1996)

Each of the four early studies (Kepner, 1991; Semke, 1984; Robb *et al.*, 1986; Sheppard, 1992) claimed that written CF did not facilitate improved written accuracy. These studies are summarised in Table 3.2 below.

Table 3.2 The early studies (pre-Truscott, 1996)

Studies	Participants	Treatment	Control group?	Effectiveness
Kepner, 1991	60 intermediate Spanish FL	1. Direct error correction 2. Content comments	Content comments?	No
Semke, 1984	141 German FL	1. Direct error correction 2. Direct error correction plus content comments 3. Error codes	Content comments?	No
Sheppard, 1992	26 upper-intermediate ESL	1. Direct error correction plus conference 2. Error codes	Content comments plus conference?	No
Robb et al., 1986	134 Japanese EFL freshmen	1. Direct error correction 2. Error codes 3. Highlighting 4. Marginal error totals	Marginal error totals?	No

There is debate about the validity of the conclusions drawn from the findings of these studies because of various design/execution shortcomings. In this regard, the Kepner (1991) study of intermediate Spanish FL learners has been critiqued on a number of levels. First, it had two treatment groups (one group that received direct error correction and the other that received content comments on their texts) but no control group of learners. Some may argue that if the content comments were not about linguistic accuracy, then the group that received these comments could be regarded as a control group. However, we are of the view that findings are only valid if the constructs are fully and unambiguously defined. Second, as Ferris (2003) explains, there was no pre-test writing task on which to determine the learners' pre-treatment level of accuracy:

> Kepner analyzed the sixth set of journal entries (out of eight total) for comparison purposes and she did not look at the first set of journal entries to see where the students started out on this type of writing. (Ferris, 2003: 60)

Consequently, the reader has no way of knowing (1) whether the two groups of learners had the same initial level of accuracy and (2) how the reported improvements were calculated. Third, the absence of detail about the conditions and controls under which the learners performed the writing tasks out-of-class and the lack of control for the length of the journal entries are additional factors that need to be considered. Irrespective of whether or not the researchers claim that the findings are evidence of learning, they need to be treated with caution. For these reasons, we are not including this study in our tally of studies for or against the effectiveness of written CF for L2 development.

The study by Semke (1984) of 141 German FL students in an American university has a similar range of design and execution issues, meaning that one needs to read the claims with caution. The first issue concerns the inclusion of the 'comments-on-content only' group as the control group. As we mentioned above in our discussion of the Kepner study, there may be different perspectives on whether such a group can really be interpreted as a control group. Second, different measurements were used for the so-called control group and the other three treatment groups. The former were measured according to the number of words that were written but the latter were measured on the basis of a ratio of number of errors to number of words written. Third, adding to this issue, as Guenette (2007) points out, there is a possibility that the findings may have been affected by the presence of an incentive for some learners. In seeking to explain 'the verve of the "content" group', Guenette (2007: 50) suggests that this group may have not been 'worried about losing points, while the other three groups probably needed to write less for fear of making too many mistakes'. These issues seem to be serious enough to caution one about the validity of the claims that have been made. Consequently, we are inclined to not include this study as evidence of the potential of written CF to facilitate L2 development.

It is similarly debatable whether Sheppard's (1992) study of 26 upper-intermediate ESL learners can be said to have included a no-correction control group and therefore be included as evidence. Again, it is questionable whether the 'comments-on-content' group can be accepted as a real control group. Even though the feedback for this group invited the learners to provide clarification when the writing was difficult to understand, it is unclear whether this may have primed them to focus on particular linguistic forms and structures. Perhaps the more concerning part of the design of this study is the one-on-one conferences each student had with the teacher. It is unclear whether the conferences between the teacher and the students in the 'comments-on-content' group avoided any discussion of difficulties in understanding meaning that may have arisen from linguistic error. Ferris (2003, 2004) has also commented that there was an absence of inter-rater reliability checks on the coding of the data. With both of these issues, it is difficult to conclude whether or not these issues critically affected the findings.

Similar cautions need to be noted with the fourth study by Robb *et al.* (1986). Ostensibly, it would seem that the fourth group (d) in this study, which received marginal feedback in the form of the total number of errors per line, should not be seen as a real control group. Truscott (2007: 261) argues that some may consider the study 'was equivalent to a controlled study because the information presented to group (d) was so limited that it could not have been helpful'. Robb *et al.* (1986) report that, even though all groups improved, there was no difference between the groups and therefore no difference between the treatment and control groups. Compared with the other studies we have discussed, this issue would seem to be less problematic than those identified in the other three studies. Thus, we are inclined to suggest less caution in this case and consider the reported findings to be potentially more valid.

Summarising the contribution of these four early studies, we are of the view that the first two should not be included as evidence of improved accuracy, and that the last two should only be accepted as evidence with a cautionary proviso. If, from what we have discussed so far, the provision of written CF makes no difference, it would seem that Krashen (1985) and Truscott (1996) may have been right when they claimed that written CF cannot be expected to facilitate L2 development. But, before we draw such a conclusion, we need to consider the growing body of more recent research that has not only managed to overcome the shortcomings of these early studies but has also reported completely different findings.

3.1.2.2 More recent studies (since Truscott, 1996)

The studies we survey in this section are summarised in Table 3.3 below.

Table 3.3 Recent studies investigating the effectiveness of written CF over time

Studies	Participants	Duration	Findings
Bitchener, 2008	75 low intermdiate ESL	6 months	Learners receiving written CF outperformed those in the control group in the immediate post-test and in the 2 months delayed post-test
Bitchener & Knoch, 2008	144 low intermediate ESL	2 months	Learners receiving written CF outperformed those in the control group in the immediate post-test and in the 2 months delayed post-test
Bitchener & Knoch, 2010a	52 low intermediate ESL	10 months	Learners receiving written CF outperformed those in the control group in the immediate post-test and in 3 delayed post-tests over 10 months
Bitchener & Knoch, 2010b	63 advanced ESL	10 weeks	Learners receiving written CF outperformed those in the control group in the immediate post-test. There were some variations across written CF groups in the 10 week delayed post-test. See Sections 3.3.1 and 3.3.? where the effects of different types of written CF are discussed.

(Continued)

Studies	Participants	Duration	Findings
Ellis *et al.*, 2008	49 intermediate EFL	10 weeks	Learners receiving written CF outperformed those in the control group in the immediate and 10 week delayed post-test
Frear, 2012	42 EFL at a Taiwan university	7 weeks	Learners receiving written CF outperformed those in control group in the immediate post-test but only the focused direct error correction group did so after 2 weeks. See Sections 3.3.1 and 3.3.2 where the effects of different types of written CF are discussed.
Guo, 2015	147 EFL at a Chinese university	19 weeks	Learners who received written CF outperformed those in the control group in the immediate post-test but not over 4 months
Rummel, 2014	72 advanced EFL at Kuwait & Laos universities	7 weeks	Learners from Laos who received written CF outperformed those who did not receive written CF over time but only learners from Kuwait who received direct error correction outperformed those who did not receive written CF over time
Sheen, 2007	91 intermediate ESL	2 months	Learners receiving written CF outperformed those in the control group in the immediate and 4 weeks delayed post-test
Sheen *et al.*, 2009	80 intermediate	9 weeks	Learners receiving written CF outperformed those in the control group in the immediate and delayed post-test
Shintani & Ellis, 2013	49 low intermediate ESL	3 weeks	Learners receiving written CF outperformed those in the control group in the immediate and 2 week delayed post-test
Shintani *et al.*, 2014	214 ESL at Japanese university	4 weeks	Learners receiving written CF outperformed those in the control group in the immediate and 2 week delayed post-test
Stefanou, 2014	89 Greek EFL	4 weeks	Learners who received written CF outperformed those who did not receive written CF over time

From the studies outlined in Table 3.3, it is clear that providing learners with written CF on even just one occasion had a beneficial effect on their written accuracy. Immediately after they had received this feedback, there was an improvement in their written accuracy, and this level of improvement, compared with no increase in accuracy for learners who did not receive any written CF, was retained over different periods of time.

Compared with the shortcomings of the early studies, those reported here are examples of appropriate design and execution and, therefore, studies that present more valid and reliable findings. Nevertheless, several critiques have been made, and these must be acknowledged. First, Truscott (2007) argued that the findings are biased, because learners who are corrected tend to shorten and simplify their writing so that they avoid making too many errors. This argument, of course, is not valid, as it overlooks the fact that (1) the accuracy rates reported in these studies were calculated as a percentage of actual use and (2) the rubric of the writing tasks (often picture descriptions) predisposed the learners to make relatively extensive use of the targeted forms. We agree that, on some occasions, learners could have used other linguistic constructions to avoid uses that they were uncertain about, but this would not have been possible on the majority of occasions.

Second, Xu (2009) suggested that the earlier studies in this set, and, by implication, others with the same characteristics, have overgeneralised the claims that can be made from their findings. Unfortunately, this claim is not supported by a close reading of the research. As Bitchener (2009) explains in his response to Xu, all claims concerning the studies were made only in relation to the targeted focus of each study. There was no intention to over-generalise the conclusions drawn about the effectiveness of written CF to linguistic forms and structures other than those targeted. In fact, mention was consistently made of the need for further research to explore the extent to which more general claims can be made about the role of written CF for treating errors in other linguistic domains. Even though the authors of these studies did not make the claims Xu suggested, all would agree that readers need to be careful to not make these leaps when reading the research. Similarly, we would caution readers of these studies not to conclude that the studies are implying that the learners have reached the level of native or near native speaker/writer competence we referred to at the beginning of Chapter 2. We explained that a period of consolidation is required for learners to convert their consciously processed explicit knowledge (demonstrated in immediate post-tests and delayed post-tests) to unconsciously retrieved and used implicit knowledge (demonstrated through consistent accuracy on multiple occasions and in multiple contexts over time).

The findings that are reported in these studies are group findings and, as such, reveal that most learners had benefitted from the written CF they had received. However, the findings do not tell us which learners failed to benefit from the feedback and, perhaps more importantly, why these learners did not improve their written accuracy over time. If we are to obtain answers to questions such as these, further research will need to include more longitudinal studies of individual learners and the progress they make, or fail to make, across the stages of information processing we discussed in Chapter 2 (namely, from initial response and attention to written CF input to consolidation and automatisation of new knowledge). One would predict that answers to these questions would then enable teachers to think about ways in which they can assist learners who fail initially to benefit from written CF. Examples of approaches that might be effective can be found in Guo (2015) and Chapter 5 of this book, where different uses of regulatory scales are described.

We would suggest that it is equally important to analyse the progress of individual learners who demonstrate improved accuracy after only one feedback treatment. It may that the existing knowledge (stored in the long-term memory) of some of the learners in the studies reviewed above was already quite well developed, and that the provision of written CF on just one occasion was enough to raise their consciousness of the required linguistic form. Also, it may be that the type of feedback that they were given was sufficiently clear for them to take their partially acquired knowledge (even if it was only in the early stages of consolidation) to the next level of development and enable them to make new hypotheses about correct target forms/structures. The extent to which other factors (including the range of individual and contextual factors we discussed in Chapter 2) might play a facilitative or inhibitive role must also form part of the design of future research into this key question.

While this body of research has produced some clear validation of the theoretical view that explicit written CF has the potential to facilitate L2 development, it has given little attention to how and why such development has occurred. In Section 3.6, we discuss what research efforts have been made to understand the cognitive processes involved in L2 development as well as the influence of individual and contextual factors on such processing.

3.2   Are Some Types of Written CF More Facilitative of L2 Development than Others?

Teachers of L2 learners have always been keen to find out whether certain types of written CF 'work' better than other types. As a result, this question has tended to dominate the research agendas of researchers and teacher-researchers since the days of behaviourist thinking. While that interest has not waned in recent decades, it would be fair to say that the motivation for investigating it has recently become more theoretically intended. As researchers become more interested in understanding *how* and *why* L2 development occurs, the question focuses more on *how* and *why* different types of written CF, each with different levels of explicitness, might enable learners to progress through the cognitive stages of information processing discussed by Gass (1997). However, most of the currently available research has focused on the effect of different types of written CF on immediate output (the product) and the extent to which its effects have been retained over time. To find out whether, in fact, any one of these types is more facilitative of L2 development than other types, researchers have compared direct error correction and less explicit types of written CF (see Section 3.2.1), direct error correction and direct error correction with more explicit types of written CF (see Section 3.2.2) and metalinguistic feedback with other types of written CF (see Section 3.2.3).

3.2.1   Studies comparing direct error correction & less explicit types of written CF

Studies comparing direct error correction and less explicit types of written CF are summarised in Table 3.4. In column 3, we indicate whether or not we believe the reported findings are valid.

Table 3.4 Studies comparing direct error correction and less explicit types of written CF

Studies	Feedback types	Effectiveness
Lalande (1982)	1. DEC 2. Indirect coding	Indirect coding more effective than direct error correction (not significant)
Semke (1984)	1. DEC 2. Content comments 3. Direct error correction & content comments 4. Indirect coding	No difference reported (design & execution issues)
Chandler (2003)	1. DEC 2. Underlining 3. Error codes	Direct error correction and underlining were more effective than error codes but no difference between error codes and underlining
Van Beuningen et al. (2008)	1. DEC 2. Indirect feedback 3. Writing practice 4. Self-correction revision	Direct error correction more effective long-term; both direct error correction and indirect feedback effective short-term
Van Beuningen et al. (2012)	1. DEC 2. Indirect feedback 3. Writing practice 4. Self-correction revision	Direct error correction more effective for grammar but indirect more effective for non-grammar items

Note: DEC = direct error correction

Lalande's (1982) study of 60 intermediate German FL learners reported an advantage for indirect feedback (coding) over direct error correction but the observed between-group difference in accuracy improvement was not statistically significant. It is also debatable whether error codes that represent metalinguistic information can rightly be included as indirect feedback. It would seem that such error codes should be classified as less explicit metalinguistic feedback. Additionally, Van Beuningen *et al.* (2012) note that 'the indirect group was engaged in more form-focused activities than the group receiving direct CF' (2012: 7). In Semke's (1984) study of 141 German FL learners, no difference was reported between direct error correction, comments, direct error correction and comments but, as Guenette (2007) points out, the groups were treated differently, and this is likely to have had an effect on the findings:

> In that study, two different types of feedback on form were compared: one group saw their errors directly corrected and another group was asked to self-correct (errors were coded) and submit a rewrite one week later. However, the groups were 'treated' differently. Because the correction group was asked to rewrite their essay rather than write a new one, students in that group wrote only half as much new material as the other groups. It is therefore very difficult to see the effect of the two different types of feedback on form – direct versus indirect corrections – because of a confounding variable (quantity of writing) that obscures the issue. In addition, correcting students' errors and asking them to recopy their essay is quite different, cognitively, from only pointing out the errors and asking them to self-correct. (Guenette, 2007: 49)

Chandler's (2003) study of 20 intermediate ESL learners investigated the effect of consecutively providing learners with direct error correction, underlining and error codes. She reported that both direct error correction and underlining were significantly more effective than error codes in reducing errors in the writing of new texts over time. No significant differences were reported between direct error correction and underlining. Nevertheless, this study cannot be compared with the other studies in this set because learners were provided with consecutive treatments rather than just one treatment. We are of the view, then, that none of these three studies can be accepted as providing evidence that direct error correction is more or less effective than indirect, less explicit forms of written CF.

On the other hand, two more recent studies by Van Beuningen *et al.* (2008, 2012) managed to avoid these design and execution issues and reported that, even though there were positive short-term effects for both direct and indirect feedback, direct error correction had a more significant long-term effect than indirect written CF. Intuitively, this finding is not surprising; as we explained in Chapter 2, one might expect more explicit forms of written CF (direct error correction) to be more effective than less explicit forms (indirect types) with learners who are in the early stages of learning and using the targeted form/structure. Even though these findings seem to be more valid and reliable, they are the only evidence we have so far. It would therefore be premature to draw any conclusions about the superiority of direct error correction over less explicit types of written CF.

3.2.2   Studies comparing direct error correction and direct error correction with more explicit types of written CF

Studies that have compared the effectiveness of direct error correction alone with direct error correction that is accompanied by more explicit types of written CF are summarised in Table 3.5 below. Combining direct error correction with more explicit types of written CF is common practice in many ESL and EFL language learning classrooms so, from a pedagogical perspective, it is important that the approach be investigated.

Table 3.5 Studies comparing direct error correction and direct error correction plus more explicit types of written CF

Study	Participants	Target form	Feedback types	Effectiveness
Bitchener et al., 2005	52 advanced ESL	Definite and indefinite articles; past simple tense; prepositions	DEC; DEC plus written ME; DEC plus written and oral ME	DEC plus oral and written ME more effective than DEC for articles and past simple tense only
Bitchener, 2008	75 low intermediate ESL	First mention indefinite article; anaphoric mention definite article	DEC; DEC plus written ME; DEC plus written and oral ME	DEC plus written and oral ME, and DEC more effective than DEC plus written ME
Bitchener & Knoch, 2008	144 low intermediate ESL	First mention indefinite article; anaphoric mention definite article	DEC; DEC plus written ME; DEC plus written and oral ME	No difference between three treatment groups

(Continued)

Study	Participants	Target form	Feedback types	Effectiveness
Bitchener & Knoch, 2010a	52 low intermediate ESL	First mention indefinite article; anaphoric mention definite article	DEC; DEC plus written ME; DEC plus written and oral ME	No difference between three treatment groups
Sheen, 2007	91 intermediate ESL	First mention indefinite article; anaphoric mention definite article	DEC; DEC plus written ME	No difference between two treatment groups in immediate post-test but DEC plus written ME more effective than DEC over 2 months
Stefanou, 2014	89 EFL in Greece	Articles with generic & specific plural referents	DEC; DEC plus written ME	No difference between the two treatment groups

Note: DEC = direct error correction; ME = metalinguistic explanation and example

In the first of these studies, Bitchener *et al.* (2005) investigated this comparison with 52 advanced ESL migrant learners over a 12-week period and reported that direct error correction plus oral metalinguistic explanation was significantly more effective than direct error correction alone for increasing accuracy in the use of the definite article and the past simple tense but not in the use of prepositions. The interactional effect of type of written CF with different types of linguistic error is discussed in Section 3.3 below. Limiting the investigation on the English article system to two of the more common functional uses (the indefinite article 'a' for first mention and the definite article 'the' for subsequent or anaphoric mentions), Bitchener (2008), Bitchener and Knoch (2008, 2010a) compared the effectiveness of direct error correction alone with direct error correction plus two other combinations: (1) written metalinguistic explanation (providing rule and example of use) with oral metalinguistic explanation and (2) written metalinguistic explanation alone. In Bitchener (2008), the low intermediate ESL migrant learners who received either direct error correction with written and oral metalinguistic explanation or direct error correction alone appeared to benefit more than those who received direct error correction plus written metalinguistic explanation over a six-month period. When Bitchener and Knoch (2008) extended the sample size with an additional 69 learners, no difference was found between the three treatment groups. It is possible that the larger sample size eliminated the difference in effect between the groups in Bitchener (2008). Therefore, while Bitchener *et al.* (2005) found the addition of metalinguistic explanation to direct error correction to be more effective than direct error correction alone, Bitchener and Knoch (2008) found no such advantage. In a more longitudinal study (10 months), Bitchener and Knoch (2010a) retained the same treatment groups. As was the case in Bitchener and Knoch (2008), no differences in effectiveness were found between the groups in this 2010 study, suggesting therefore that direct error correction plus more explicit types of written CF (including metalinguistic explanation) were no more beneficial to the learners than direct error correction alone.

Intuitively, one might have expected more explicit feedback to be advantageous for low intermediate learners. However, several explanations might be offered to account for this result. First, as low proficiency learners, they may have had a more limited working memory capacity than more advanced learners, and therefore have been less able to cope with cognitive load and process metalinguistic explanations and apply this information to the errors they had made (see Chapter 2 for a discussion of the potential effect of these factors on cognitive processing). Second, the limited information given in the metalinguistic explanation (rule and example) may have failed to provide enough detail for such learners. Third, mediating factors such as those we discussed in Chapter 2 may have limited their processing of the feedback. Until more research focuses on the effect of such variables on different stages of the cognitive processing, we will not know the extent of their influence.

In her recent study, Stefanou (2014) also found no difference between direct error correction, on the one hand, and direct error correction plus metalinguistic explanation on the other. Commenting on this unexpected outcome, she wrote:

> Interestingly, however, the results in the ... study provide no clear evidence for the benefit of complementing direct written corrections with metalinguistic information. In the comparison between the two conditions, the differences between them reached the required level of significance only for one test component (the generic-reference part of the picture description test). However, on that particular test, a significant imbalance was identified between the two groups in terms of their pre-test performance. Thus, the results obtained did not allow for one of the two written CF groups to be characterised as more effective than the other. (Stefanou, 2014: 209)

Sheen's (2007) study of the effectiveness of direct error correction alone and direct error correction plus written metalinguistic explanation also found no difference between the two types of written CF in the immediate post-test but, in the delayed post-test (two months later), she found that direct error correction plus written metalinguistic explanation was more effective than direct error correction alone. As Sheen suggests, the passage of time may have been the critical factor. From these findings, it is clear, then, that further research would be needed if a firm conclusion is to be drawn.

It is possible that a separation of feedback approaches (for example, separating direct error correction and metalinguistic explanation) might yield more consistent findings than the combinations that have been reported on in this section even though such an approach may be less ecologically valid in non-experimental classroom contexts. As we will see in the next section, several studies have in fact adopted this approach and compared the effectiveness of metalinguistic explanation and other types of written CF.

3.2.3   Studies comparing metalinguistic feedback and other types of written CF

Five recent studies have investigated the relative effectiveness of metalinguistic explanation and other types of written CF. These are summarised in Table 3.6 below.

Table 3.6 Studies comparing metalinguistic feedback & other types of written CF

Studies	Participants	Target form	Feedback types	Effectiveness
Bitchener & Knoch, 2010b	63 advanced ESL	First mention indefinite article; anaphoric mention definite article	1. Written ME 2. Underlining/ circling 3. Written & oral ME 4. Control	No difference between 3 treatment groups in immediate post-test; both ME groups outperformed the indirect underlining/ circling group over time (10 weeks)
Guo (2015)	147 Chinese EFL	Regular & irregular past tense; prepositions indicating space	1. DEC 2. DEC & written ME 3. Written ME 4. Underlining 5. Error code 6. Control	Groups 1–3 outperformed groups 4–5 and the control. There was no difference between groups 1–3
Rummel (2014)	72 advanced EFL at Kuwait and Laos universities	Past simple tense; present perfect tense	1. DEC 2. Indirect error correction 3. Written ME 4. Control	No difference between three treatment groups for Laos learners but Kuwaiti DEC group outperformed the other treatment groups

(Continued)

Studies	Participants	Target form	Feedback types	Effectiveness
Shintani & Ellis, 2013	49 low intermediate ESL	Indefinite article	1. DEC 2. ME 3. Control	ME group outperformed DEC group in immediate post-test but not in delayed post-test (2 weeks)
Shintani et al., 2014	214 EFL at a Japanese university	Indefinite article; hypothetical conditional	1. DEC 2. DEC plus revision 3. ME 4. ME plus revision 5. Control	The DEC group outperformed the ME group in the post-test only (2 weeks)

Note: DEC = direct error correction; ME = metalinguistic explanation

In their study of 63 advanced ESL freshmen at a university in the USA, Bitchener and Knoch (2010b) compared written metalinguistic explanation, written and oral metalinguistic explanation and indirect underlining/ circling of errors in the use of the same two functional uses of the English article system that they investigated in earlier studies. In the immediate post-test, they reported no difference in effectiveness between the three treatment groups but, in the delayed post-test (after 10 weeks), they found that both metalinguistic groups outperformed the indirect underlining/ circling group. The passage of time may have been the critical factor in this finding, a factor that was also referred to by Sheen (2007) to explain the delayed effect in her study. Similarly, Guo (2015), in her study of 147 Chinese EFL learners, found that the learners who received more explicit types of written CF (direct error correction; metalinguistic explanation; direct error correction plus metalinguistic explanation) outperformed those who received the less explicit types of feedback (underlining and error code) and that there was no difference between the three most explicit types. There was also no difference between the effectiveness of direct error correction and written metalinguistic explanation in treating errors in the use of the indefinite article by 49 low intermediate ESL learners in a study by Shintani and Ellis (2013), even though, in the immediate post-test, the metalinguistic explanation group outperformed the direct error correction group. This finding was also corroborated by Rummel (2014), who reported no difference between the direct error correction, metalinguistic explanation and indirect feedback groups in treating the past simple tense and present perfect aspect errors of her Laotian learners. However, it is to be noted that her Kuwaiti learners benefitted more from direct error correction than the other two treatment conditions. Rummel suggests that the difference between the learners' beliefs about what constitutes effective feedback and the difference in teaching and learning approaches in Laos and Kuwait may explain the difference. Similar to the Laos findings are those of another EFL group (at a Japanese university) in the study by Shintani *et al.* (2014), where direct error correction was found to be more effective than metalinguistic explanation after two weeks. In further comparing these types of feedback when revision was added, the study found that the direct error correction group with revision continued to outperform the metalinguistic explanation with revision group. These findings contradict the findings of Shintani and Ellis (2013), referred to above, but, as the researchers suggest, direct error correction may be more helpful to lower proficiency learners for complex structures like the hypothetical conditional.

As we said in the previous section, a range of additional factors appear to have played a part in all of these findings, with different sets of factors producing different outcomes. The contradictory findings of not only the studies in this set but also those in the two earlier sets on different types of written CF (Sections 3.2.1 and 3.2.2) tend to suggest that attempts to find out whether a particular type of written CF is likely to be more effective than other types may not be the best question for us to be asking. More meaningful answers about the role of different types of written CF might be reached if future research were to focus on those about the interactional effect of feedback types and other variables such as those referred to above (e.g. linguistic focus and level of understanding of the written CF, individual and contextual factors). In particular, future research would do well to examine the moderating effect of individual factors like attentional capacity in relation to different stages of information (written CF) processing discussed in Chapter 2, long-term memory retrieval, motivation at different processing stages (both initially on receipt of the first written CF episode and over time when retrieving knowledge from the long-term memory), processing in the working memory and producing output on multiple occasions. In short, more nuanced, more fine-tuned questions may lead to more consistent findings and more useful conclusions.

3.3   Is Written CF More Effective in Targeting Certain Linguistic Error Domains/Categories?

We have seen in Section 3.1 above that there is growing evidence that written CF has the potential to facilitate L2 development, but the extent to which it can effectively target the range of linguistic errors that learners make is less clear. Because the development of syntax, morphology and lexis requires an understanding of form, of meaning and of use in relation to other words and other parts of the language system, learners may need to focus their attention on more than just one linguistic element each time they hypothesise the correct form or structure to use. It has also been explained (Huebner, 1983; Young, 1996) that one form or structure may be more difficult to learn than another and that the different form/structure may be acquired at different developmental stages (Pienemann, 1998; Shintani *et al.*, 2014). Thus, as Ferris (1999) has argued, some forms/structures may potentially be more 'treatable' than others. Over the years, it has been suggested (e.g. Ferris, 2002, 2003; Bitchener & Ferris, 2012) that rule-based forms/structures (for example, the regular simple past tense that requires the added suffix –ed) may be more 'treatable' than item-based forms/structures (that is, those that are not governed by rules like, for example, the irregular simple past tense). To some extent, the written CF research addresses this claim but it does not account for the fact that some rule-based forms/structures may be more inherently complex than others (for example, how the linguistic environment in which they are used may increase the range of linguistic elements that learners need to attend to when forming hypotheses).

In this section, we survey studies that have focused on specific linguistic error categories and, in Section 3.4, we examine the extent to which focused or targeted feedback (that is, one, two or three forms/structures on a single occasion) may be more effective than unfocused or comprehensive feedback. In Table 3.7, we identify the error categories that were targeted in each study and show the extent to which written CF was effective in helping learners improve the accuracy with which they used the targeted form/structure.

Table 3.7 The effectiveness of written CF for developing accuracy in the use of linguistic forms and structures

Studies	Linguistic focus	Findings
Bitchener *et al.*, 2005	Articles, past simple tense, prepositions	Effective for articles and past simple tense
Bitchener, 2008; Bitchener & Knoch, 2008, 2009b, 2010a, 2010b	Indefinite article 'a' for first mention & definite article 'the' for subsequent or anaphoric mentions	Effective for both
Ellis *et al.*, 2008	Indefinite article 'a' for first mention & definite article 'the' for subsequent or anaphoric mentions	Effective for both
Frear, 2012	Regular and irregular verb forms	Effective for regular but not irregular forms

(Continued)

Studies	Linguistic focus	Findings
Guo, 2015	Regular and irregular past tense; prepositions indicating space	Effective for irregular past tense but not over time
Rummel, 2014	Simple past tense & present perfect tense	Effective for both
Sheen, 2007	Indefinite article 'a' for first mention & definite article 'the' for subsequent or anaphoric mentions	Effective for both
Shintani & Ellis, 2013	Indefinite article	Effective in immediate post-test but not over two weeks
Shintani et al., 2014	Indefinite article & hypothetical conditional	Not effective for indefinite article. Effective for hypothetical conditional but not over time
Stefanou, 2014	Articles with generic & specific plural referents	Effective for both

The extent to which written CF can help learners understand how the English article system works and enable them to use this knowledge accurately when revising and writing new texts has been the focus of much of the published written CF research. Bitchener *et al.* (2005) investigated the effect of written CF on three linguistic error categories (the use of the English article system, the simple past tense and prepositions) over a 12-week period and found it to be effective for helping learners improve their accuracy in using both the article system and the simple past tense but not in their use of prepositions. Even though Bitchener *et al.* (2005) found that written CF was effective in targeting article use in general, Bitchener (2008) pointed out that this finding did not examine the extent to which it had effectively targeted different functional uses of the English article system. Thus, Bitchener and Knoch (2008), Sheen (2007) and Ellis *et al.* (2008) developed a series of studies to investigate this issue. Studies by Bitchener (2008) and Bitchener and Knoch (2008, 2009b, 2010a, 2010b) investigated two frequent functional uses of the English article system: the use of the indefinite article 'a/an' for first mention and the use of the definite article for subsequent or anaphoric mentions. Each of these studies found that written CF is able to help learners improve the accuracy with which they use the articles for both functions and that it was effective for both intermediate and low intermediate learners as well as for advanced learners (Bitchener & Knoch, 2010b). Ellis *et al.* (2008) and Sheen (2007) also found that written CF is effective in targeting these frequently used functions of the English article system.

In their recently published studies, Shintani and Ellis (2013) and Shintani *et al.* (2014) explain that because learners have a tendency to overgeneralise the use of the definite article, it is difficult to know whether they have acquired the definite article for specific grammatical functions. They argue that 'restricting the analysis to "a" for first mention allows for a more reliable scoring of the effect of instruction on acquisition' (Shintani & Ellis, 2013: 292). Both studies by Shintani and colleagues found that written CF was not able to help learners in these studies improve their use of the indefinite article over time (two weeks) but, in the first of these two studies, they reported that the provision of metalinguistic explanation (but not direct CF) facilitated improved accuracy in the immediate post-test. As a result of interviews with the learners, they suggest that the learners had given less attention to the indefinite article than the other targeted structure in their study – the hypothetical conditional:

> Given the demands imposed on the learners' processing capacity by the need to recall and encode the propositional content of a text, they found their attention on the structure that was more salient and more semantically important in both the input provided by the task passages and their output (i.e. the hypothetical conditional). (Shintani *et al.*, 2014: 124)

To further unravel the conditions under which written CF may be able to help learners develop their knowledge and use of the English article system, further research on article use would be best to target separately the indefinite article 'a', the definite article 'the' and the zero article because it seems from these studies that each article and each functional use may respond differently to written CF.

Some attention has also been given to the effectiveness of written CF for helping learners improve the accuracy with which they use the simple past tense. Bitchener *et al.* (2005) and Rummel (2014) found it was effective but they did not make a distinction between the regular simple past tense (a rule-based form requiring the suffix –ed) and the irregular simple past tense, which, like item-based lexical items, does not draw upon a single rule for all uses. Intuitively, one would expect learners to have less difficulty in mastering the regular simple past tense. Frear (2012) reports that this was indeed the finding of his comparison between regular and irregular uses of the simple past tense over seven weeks.

It is not surprising that prepositions as a single category were less responsive to written CF in Bitchener *et al.* (2005) because there are many prepositional sub-categories (for example, prepositions indicating space, time, direction and so on) and some of these have specific rules for specific functions while others can be accurately used for various functions, depending on the linguistic environment and, sometimes, an individual's stylistic preference. Thus, it may be that written CF is more effective in targeting some of these sub-categories than others. One study (Guo, 2015) that investigated the effectiveness of written CF for treating errors in the use of prepositions indicating space found that written CF was not effective for Chinese EFL learners. Further research that replicates this study and that compares different preposition sub-categories would be needed before any conclusions are drawn. Similarly, further research would be needed to investigate whether or not written CF can help learners develop accuracy in their use of other sub-categories of preposition.

Even though it would seem that rule-based forms/structures are potentially more treatable than item-based forms/structures, it is important to realise that some rule-based forms/structures are more complex than the two we have reviewed so far. The hypothetical conditional, for example, which expresses the hypothetical outcome of an event that did not occur, can be regarded as more difficult to acquire because its structure is complex both syntactically and semantically. As Celce-Murcia and Larsen-Freeman (1999) explain, an accurate use of the hypothetical conditional requires knowledge of the tense-aspect system, modal auxilaries and negation, and as Izumi et al. (1999) add, it requires learners to encode two functions, namely, hypotheticality and time reference (past and future). Clearly, then, more attentional capacity is required by learners when using it. Less explicit types of written CF may not be sufficient for relatively low proficiency learners who need written CF with more explanation and illustration; such learners may benefit more from metalinguistic CF than from other types of feedback. In their comparison of the indefinite article and the hypothetical conditional (the latter assumed to be more complex), Shintani et al. (2014) found that accuracy gains in the use of the hypothetical conditional were not sustained over time. When comparing this finding with the retention reported over time for the other linguistic forms/structures in earlier studies reviewed in this section, the researchers put the difference down to the difference in rule complexity between their study and that of other studies.

As we can see from this overview, written CF studies have focused on only a few linguistic error categories and on each occasion effectiveness in terms of improved output (the product) has been the focus of attention rather than an investigation into whether or not cognitive processing during internalisation, modification and consolidation phases of development operates differently according to the linguistic focus of the written CF.

In terms of both foci (process and product), much more research is therefore needed on a wider range of linguistic error categories/domains and functional uses. This is particularly important because studies that have targeted specific functional uses of a form/structure may not always yield similar findings to studies targeting other functional uses. Investigations of the extent to which written CF can focus on the development of more complex structures also need to be designed. In carrying out such studies, it may be important to find out whether written CF is more effective if it targets a single form/structure at a time rather than two or more on a single occasion. As we will see in the following section, there is a body of research that has started to look at this question.

3.4   The Relative Effectiveness of Focused and Unfocused Written CF

In each of the early studies (referred to in Section 3.1.2.1), feedback on a single occasion was given to learners on a wide range of error categories and, as such, have been categorised as either unfocused or comprehensive studies. More recent studies of language learners have investigated the effectiveness of either 'highly focused' feedback on only one targeted category of error or 'less focused CF' on a limited number of targeted error categories (Ellis *et al.*, 2008: 356). While some teachers of language learning classes provide more comprehensive feedback, others are of the view that a targeted approach is more facilitative of L2 development. As we have seen in Chapter 2, a more targeted approach may make more sense, theoretically, for lower proficiency learners, as it reduces their cognitive load and is arguably more likely to engage the level of attention required to process new information. It may be that more advanced learners are able to attend to, process and use a wider range of input on a single occasion. To what extent, then, does the published research indicate that either of these approaches may be more facilitative of learning than the other?

3.4.1   Studies of focused written CF

Each of the studies presented in Table 3.8 below targeted only one, two or three error categories at a time, and found that a single written CF episode facilitated improved accuracy. It may have been that a reduction in the attentional load facilitated development in each case but until sufficient studies compare focused and unfocused feedback we will not know if this is the case. The extent to which the interaction of other factors/variables might impact on any benefits of the targeted approach is also an important question for on-going research.

3.4.2   Studies of unfocused written CF

Only three studies (Truscott & Hsu, 2008; Van Beuningen *et al.*, 2008, 2012) have investigated the effectiveness of providing written CF on a comprehensive range of error types (from grammatical form and structure to lexical and punctuation errors). Although the four early studies (in Section 3.1.2.2) provided comprehensive written CF, we are not including them in this discussion because of the design and execution issues referred to earlier.

Table 3.8 Studies of focused written CF

Studies	Participants	Error categories
Bitchener *et al.*, 2005	Post-intermediate ESL	Definite article; past simple tense; prepositions
Bitchener, 2008	Low intermediate ESL	2 functional uses of English article system: indefinite article (first mention), definite article (anaphoric mention)
Bitchener & Knoch, 2008	Low intermediate ESL	2 functional uses of English article system: indefinite article (first mention), definite article (anaphoric mention)
Bitchener & Knoch, 2009a	Low intermediate ESL	2 functional uses of English article system: indefinite article (first mention), definite article (anaphoric mention)
Bitchener & Knoch, 2010	Low intermediate ESL	2 functional uses of English article system: indefinite article (first mention), definite article (anaphoric mention)
Bitchener & Knoch, 2010b	Advanced ESL	2 functional uses of English article system: indefinite article (first mention), definite article (anaphoric mention)
Guo, 2015	Pre-intermediate EFL (China)	Regular and irregular past simple tense; prepositions indicating space
Rummel, 2014	Advanced EFL (Kuwait & Laos)	Past simple tense; present perfect tense
Sheen, 2007	Intermediate ESL	2 functional uses of English article system: indefinite article (first mention), definite article (anaphoric mention)
Ellis *et al.*, 2008	Intermediate EFL (Japan)	2 functional uses of English article system: indefinite article (first mention), definite article (anaphoric mention)
Shintani & Ellis, 2013	Low intermediate ESL	Indefinite article
Shintani *et al.*, 2014	Advanced EFL (Japan)	Indefinite article, hypothetical conditional
Stefanou, 2014	Advanced EFL (Greece)	Articles with generic & specific plural referents

It can be seen that very little research has investigated the effectiveness of unfocused written CF and, from the studies that have (see Table 3.9), the findings are contradictory. Even though each of these studies was generally well designed, there are limitations in the parameters of the Truscott and Hsu study and questions that can be asked about some of the design and execution characteristics of the Van Beuningen *et al.* study that mean it is too early to draw any firm conclusions. In the Truscott and Hsu study, only one form of feedback was investigated, and that was an indirect underlining of errors. Concerning the Van Beuningen studies, questions may be asked about (1) whether the researchers controlled for additional input between giving feedback and the one week delay in administering the immediate post-test, and (2) whether the self-correction group was a real control group given that the learners' attention was focused on accuracy when doing the self-correction. Theoretically, it may be argued that learners with a more developed knowledge of and practice in using the forms/structures on which they receive written CF may benefit from a wider range of feedback at any one time. On the other hand, learners with only partially developed knowledge and opportunities for application may need more targeted feedback, and a more sustained approach to attend to and consciously process the feedback. Further research that does this by comparing learners at different proficiency levels may be able to address this possibility. Irrespective of whether focused written CF alone or unfocused written CF alone is effective in helping learners improve their linguistic accuracy, the question about whether one of these approaches is more effective than another can only be answered if the two are compared within a single research design.

Table 3.9 Studies of unfocused written CF

Studies	Participants	Error categories	Effectiveness
Truscott & Hsu, 2008	47 high intermediate ESL	All grammatical, spelling and punctuation errors	Not effective
Van Beuningen et al., 2008	62 secondary school Dutch FL	All grammatical forms/structures (e.g. tenses; singular-plural; word order), incomplete sentences, lexical choice, word omission or inclusion, spelling, punctuation, capitalisation	Effective
Van Beuningen et al., 2012	268 secondary school Dutch FL	All grammatical forms/structures (e.g. tenses; singular-plural; word order), incomplete sentences, lexical choice, word omission or inclusion, spelling, punctuation, capitalisation	Effective

3.4.3 Studies of focused and unfocused written CF

Two studies (Ellis *et al.*, 2008; Sheen *et al.*, 2009) have attempted to find out whether focused written CF is more effective than unfocused written CF. Ellis *et al.* (2008) compared the effectiveness of providing 49 Japanese male intermediate EFL learners with focused or unfocused written CF. The focused group received direct error correction on article errors only while the unfocused group received correction on the article errors as well as other error categories. The researchers reported that both types of feedback were equally effective. However, they acknowledged first that the two types of feedback were insufficiently distinguished from one another, with article errors being highly represented in both and, second, that further research would need to address this type of construct issue.

As a result, Sheen *et al.* (2009) investigated the effects of focused and unfocused written CF on both a single grammatical target (the English article system) and a broader range of grammatical structures (articles, copula 'be', regular past tense, irregular past tense, prepositions). While they reported that focused written CF on the English article system alone was more effective than unfocused written CF, caution needs to be taken when interpreting these findings because, as the researchers themselves admit, the written CF that the unfocused group received was not systematic; some of the errors were corrected but others were not corrected.

Because of the construct issues in both studies, it is not possible to draw any conclusions about the superiority of focused or unfocused written CF for L2 development. Even though the studies that have investigated the effectiveness of a focused approach report consistent findings on the benefit of the approach, it is important that further research compare the two approaches so that theoretical predictions about cognitive load being critical for lower proficiency learners can be validated. At the pedagogical level, teachers would find it helpful to know whether the time-consuming comprehensive approach is worth the time they invest or whether the more targeted approach, less likely to take as much time to implement, has greater potential for L2 development.

3.5 The Moderating Effect of Individual and Contextual Factors

In Chapter 2, we explained the potential of individual and contextual factors to moderate (1) whether or not learners respond and attend to written CF and (2) the progress that they make across the information processing stages outlined in the model designed by Gass (1997).

Understanding whether certain individual and contextual factors have the potential to mediate progress (namely, the extent to which they might have a facilitative or impeding effect on L2 development) may help us understand why some learners develop their L2 knowledge and capacity for accurate use more easily than others, and why some learners fail to learn from the feedback provided. To date, very little attention has been given within the cognitive perspective to the effect of such factors on learners' use of written CF. In the following sections, we provide an overview of what has been investigated: individual cognitive factors (language analytic ability, grammatical sensitivity and knowledge of metalanguage); individual and contextual factors (e.g. beliefs and attitudes about written CF as well as prior learning experiences in different contexts).

3.5.1   Research on individual cognitive factors

One individual cognitive factor that has been investigated is language analytic ability (Skehan, 1998), that is, two components (grammatical sensitivity and inductive language learning ability) of Carroll's (1981) definition of aptitude. Sheen (2007) investigated the potential of language analytic ability to mediate the effects of written CF on the acquisition of articles by 91 adult intermediate ESL learners from a range of first language backgrounds. Conducted over a four-week period, the study found that there was a significantly positive association between gains in accuracy and learners' aptitude for language analysis. She discovered that language analytic ability was more strongly related to acquisition by those who received direct metalinguistic feedback than by those who received direct error correction. Intuitively, one would expect learners with high language analytic ability to engage more in the kind of cognitive comparison that is hypothesised to result in learning. Similarly, it is understandable that direct metalinguistic feedback should benefit analytically strong language learners more than analytically weak learners because they would be more likely to make an effective use of such feedback. These explanations confirm the advantage that Schmidt (2001) assigned to learners who understand with metalinguistic awareness and, as this study indicates, such awareness would seem more likely to take place with learners who have a greater capacity to engage in an analysis of the information provided in written CF. These findings were further corroborated in Sheen's (2011) study of 91 intermediate ESL learners, 31 of whom received direct error correction, 32 direct error correction plus metalinguistic explanation and 28 no feedback on English articles.

Extending the work of Sheen, Stefanou (2014) in her study of 89 Greek intermediate EFL learners, investigated the possible impact of three individual learner cognitive factors (inductive language learning ability, grammatical sensitivity and knowledge of metalanguage) on learners' ability to benefit from direct error correction and direct error correction plus metalinguistic explanation. She found that the learners' grammatical sensitivity and knowledge of metalanguage had a positive effect on the extent to which they benefitted from the feedback they received. Learners who received direct error correction alone and who had a higher level of grammatical sensitivity and a more thorough knowledge of metalanguage were more able to improve their article use. When metalinguistic information was also provided, the accuracy improvement of the learners did not seem to be affected by their level of grammatical sensitivity or familiarity with metalinguistic knowledge. Stefanou concludes, then, that written CF with metalinguistic information may 'neutralize any differences that may exist between learners in terms of their cognitive abilities' (Stefanou, 2014: 211).

Using think-aloud protocols in a follow-up study, Stefanou (2014) investigated the cognitive processes that may have been activated as a result of the written CF the learners had received. She found that the learners' attention to the errors they had made in article use was facilitated equally well by both types of written CF but that the level of awareness the learners developed varied according to the type of feedback received – an effect we theorised may be the case (see Chapter 2). Direct error correction alone generated awareness at the lower level of noticing but, with metalinguistic explanation, awareness was observed at the higher level of understanding. The study also found that for those who received direct error correction alone, there were no links between learners' awareness and their level of inductive language learning ability, grammatical sensitivity and knowledge of metalinguistic explanation whereas, for those who also received metalinguistic explanation, these variables seemed to have been counteracted by the stronger effect of more explicit written CF.

The final part of Stefanou's study employed stimulated recall to investigate the processes that the learners employed in their article use. It found that they drew upon translation from their L1 (and often wrote with no rules in mind) and considered issues such as plurality and the distinction between generic and specific reference. Learners with high measures of the three individual learner factors were found to be 'more likely to explain their article choices with reference to grammar rules, pay more attention to the grammar of their sentences and use appropriate terminology in their reports' (2014: 214).

Of all the written CF studies reviewed in this chapter, Stefanou's investigations are possibly the most forward-thinking in that they not only focus on learners' output as product but also on their processing of written CF. As more research embarks upon this kind of agenda, the more likely we are to receive answers to questions about (1) why some learners benefit from written CF and others do not and (2) how and why learners respond to, process and use the feedback they are given. Important as answers to these questions are, the impact of individual learner affective and motivational factors is, arguably, even more important because, without a desire to attend to and respond to feedback when it is given, learners are less likely to cognitively engage with the written CF input they receive.

3.5.2   Research on individual affective and contextual factors

We explained in Chapter 2 that attitudes and beliefs about written CF are not synonyms even though they are often consider together in the literature. Attitudes can be informed by a number of individual, social and contextual factors and one of these can be learners' beliefs about what works best for them. With regard to written CF, learners may have preferences about the type of written CF they receive and these beliefs may be informed by their prior learning experiences, for example, the teaching and learning focus of the contexts they have studied in and the degree of success they feel they have had in understanding and applying the information supplied in the feedback that they were given in these contexts. Two studies have explored the potential of these factors to impact upon the effectiveness of written for L2 development.

In Bitchener and Knoch (2008), 144 learners were assigned to two different groups. The first group of 75 comprised, for the most part, East Asian learners who were used to receiving written CF and to focusing on accuracy in their L2 classrooms. The second group of 69 learners were migrants who had recently arrived in New Zealand from a diverse range of language learning backgrounds and who reported in their bio questionnaires that they seldom received the type of formal classroom instruction (including written CF) that they were currently receiving. In this study, errors in the use of two functional uses of the English article system were targeted with written CF. It was hypothesised that group one would respond more favourably to written CF than the learners in the second group. However, this was not the case. There was no difference in overall performance between the two groups. This was a surprising result because it had been expected that the first group would be more likely to attend to the written CF they were given and then respond to it with greater accuracy than the learners in group two. Accounting for this result, the researchers suggested that the two groups may have not been as tightly categorised as needed to investigate the research question. In other words, neither of the two groups may have included learners exclusively from the categorised background defining each group: to some extent, there may have been an overlap in the membership of the two groups. It is possible that learners in group two may have had more formal exposure to a focus on form and written accuracy than they had indicated in their background bio-statements.

Also investigating the potential of prior learning contexts to influence L2 learning but with a particular focus on the extent to which learners' beliefs about written CF might help them improve the accuracy of their writing, Rummel (2014) provided 72 EFL learners (30 from Kuwait and 42 from Laos) with written CF on errors in their use of the past simple tense and the present perfect tense. In this study, only some of the learners received the type of written CF they said that they thought would be most useful. Rummel found that learners' beliefs about the type of written CF they considered to be most helpful for improving their L2 knowledge (measured in terms of a reduction in errors in new pieces of writing) did not seem to have this effect for the Kuwaiti learners whereas it did have an effect on the accuracy performance of learners from Laos. Of the eight Kuwaiti learners who reduced their errors, all of them had received direct error correction, but only one of these had received his preferred type of feedback (i.e. indirect). This would seem to suggest that regardless of their stated beliefs, direct error correction was a stronger influence than written CF preference. By contrast, the learners from Laos (across all feedback groups) were able to improve the accuracy of their writing after receiving the type of written CF they believed was most helpful (i.e. indirect). Rummel refers to the learners' past learning experiences in her interpretation of the difference between the two groups of learners. She suggests that their prior language learning background may have impacted on their uptake of written CF because most of the learners from Laos who preferred indirect feedback had had previous experience with that type of feedback. For the Kuwaiti learners, she suggests that the lack of effect of beliefs on uptake could have occurred because those who claimed to prefer indirect or metalinguistic explanation had had less experience with receiving that type of feedback and may not have been sufficiently adept at using it.

While the studies reported in this section have been limited in number, the questions they have introduced have been important for advancing our understanding of how individual factors may potentially moderate cognitive processes and output. Further investigations of this type must be included in the agendas of written CF researchers. It will be seen in Chapter 4 that studies conducted within the sociocultural perspective have also focused on these and related variables.

3.6 Concluding Remarks

The aim of this chapter was to review and critically assess the written CF research in terms of its contribution to L2 development. We explained that most of the research had been more pedagogically motivated and that the roots of this focus could be found in the early behaviourist perspectives informing early feedback studies. Therefore, this perspective has tended to shape the research questions that have been investigated. We explained how teachers and researchers were particularly interested in finding answers to questions about whether a certain aspect of written CF practice is more effective than another aspect for L2 development. But, asking whether or not one type of written CF (e.g. indirect, direct, metalinguistic feedback) is more effective than another tends to suggest that one type might be expected to be more effective than another. As the findings of the studies reviewed in this chapter have shown, there is not one type of written CF that can be identified as the most effective for all learners on all occasions. Rather, the findings have suggested that the type of written CF that is most likely to be effective for a particular learners will vary according to a range of additional factors/variables, such as those identified in this chapter and in Chapter 2.

As well as investigating whether certain types of written CF might be more effective than other types, questions have also focused on whether written CF might be more effective if it targets certain linguistic errors or if it targets only one or a few errors at a time. Although there is insufficient evidence for categorical answers to these questions, there are some emerging patterns. For example, it would seem that simple, rule-based forms/structures might be more easily targeted with written CF than more complex, rule-based forms/structures (because more than one linguistic element is usually involved in the processing of such forms/structures) and more idiosyncratic, item-based forms/structures for which there are no rules that can be applied across all types. The question of whether focused or unfocused written CF is more effective needs further examination. This can only be done if the two approaches are examined within a single research design.

We have explained that the findings of many of the studies investigating these questions have been conflicting. This does not necessarily signal design or execution flaws: rather, it can be the result of an interaction of different factors/variables. Thus, one type of written CF (e.g. indirect written CF) might be effective for one group of learners (e.g. advanced) but not another group of learners (e.g. less advanced). It might be that another type of written CF (e.g. direct or metalinguistic written CF) might be more effective for less advanced learners. Equally, unfocused written CF might be effective for one group of learners (e.g. advanced) but not for another group (e.g. less advanced). This suggests the need for questions that investigate the interaction of a range of factors/variables.

For the most part, the focus on whether certain variables or factors are more or less facilitative of L2 development has been examined in terms of improved accuracy output, produced at certain early on in the learner's developmental journey. Until recently, little attention has been given to investigations of the information processing that occurs from written CF input to modified output. Research that also focuses on this agenda will aid our understanding of why some learners benefit from written CF while others do not appear to not benefit from it. It is this line of enquiry that will reveal at which points along the information processing continuum from input to output a learner's conscious processing and hypothesising successfully moves from one stage to another or breaks down at one of the stages. While the research to date has shown that written CF, as explicit input, has the potential, under certain conditions at least, to help learners develop their explicit L2 knowledge through consciously attending to the information it supplies and use it accurately on subsequent occasions, less is known empirically about why learners are able to progress (or fail to progress) from one stage of processing to another and how individual and contextual factors may moderate the processing of written CF input. In Chapter 6, we consider a range of specific questions that will help us gain further empirical insight into the potential of written CF for L2 development.

4 The Sociocultural Perspective on Written CF for L2 Development

4.0 Introduction

Sociocultural theory of mind, abbreviated to SCT, is a relatively recent theoretical framework in applied linguistics research, including research on L2 writing and written CF. Its application to applied linguistics research can be traced to the mid-1980s, with the publication of studies by Frawley and Lantolf (e.g. Frawley & Lantolf, 1985), which investigated how L2 speakers use language (the L2) to mediate their performance when completing difficult tasks. Since then, a growing number of scholars have employed the theory in research on L2 learning, teaching and testing to answer questions of how and why humans learn and use an L2. More recently, the theory has also been applied to investigations of CF delivered by teaches and peers. Ellis (2010: 160), in fact, has suggested that 'the theory best equipped to explain CF as a sociocognitive phenomenon is a sociocultural theory'. These sentiments have been echoed by Lee (2014), who laments the dearth of discussion on teacher feedback which are informed by sociocultural perspectives, and in particular activity theory, a theory derived from sociocultural theory.

In this chapter, we present what SCT has to say about written CF and what kind of feedback is likely to lead to L2 development. We begin with an overview of SCT, noting the importance the theory attributes to human interaction, what aspects of the interaction are highlighted, and perhaps more importantly, how it views development. Following this overview, we focus on two sets of interrelated constructs in SCT, constructs which are of most relevance to a discussion of written CF. The first set – the Zone of Proximal Development (ZPD) and scaffolding – frames our subsequent discussion on traits of effective written CF. The second set – mediation and tools – is pertinent to considerations of how feedback is delivered and processed. The discussion then turns to the notion of activity, which has emerged as a theory in its own right: activity theory (AT). AT proposes that human behaviour, such as learners' responses to written CF, needs to be considered holistically, by taking individual and context-specific factors into account simultaneously.

Our discussion of these key constructs begins with an explanation of what these constructs mean. We then discuss specifically how they relate to written CF. Our overall aim is to show how SCT and AT can be employed to explain how and why written CF may contribute to L2 development of an individual learner or a group of learners.

4.1 Sociocultural Theory of Mind (SCT): An Overview

Sociocultural theory of mind is based on the work of Soviet psychologist Lev Vygotsky (1978, 1981). It was further developed by his Soviet colleagues (e.g. Leontiev, 1978), by Western scholars in the field of psychology and education (e.g. Engeström, 1987, 2001; Rogoff, 1990; Wells, 1999; Wertsch, 1991) as well as scholars in SLA (e.g. Lantolf, 2000; Lantolf & Thorne, 2006; Swain, 2000, 2006a; Swain et al., 2011). It should be noted at the outset that SCT is not a theory of second language learning but rather a psychological theory that explains the development of complex human cognitive abilities. The theory explains how biologically endowed mental capacities (e.g. memory, involuntary attention) develop into uniquely human higher order cognitive capacities (e.g. intentional memory, voluntary attention, ability to plan, logic), over which humans, unlike other species, can exercise control.

The key premise in sociocultural theory is that the development of these higher order cognitive capacities occurs in highly contextualised interactions between an expert member of the community (an adult, or a knowledgeable peer) and a novice (a child, or a less knowledgeable peer) (Vygotsky, 1978, 1981). These interactions are mediated by artefacts (or tools) that may be physical (e.g. computers) or symbolic (e.g. gestures, language). Of the symbolic tools, language is perhaps the most important tool because it enables dialogue to take place.

What distinguishes SCT from other psychological theories of cognitive development (e.g. Piaget, 1977) is that it views the direction of development from the social to the individual; that is, it proposes that cognitive functions appear first in social interactions between humans, and subsequently become internalised within the individual. It should also be noted that internalisation is not merely a process whereby the novice simply imitates the expert (Lantolf & Thorne, 2006), but rather a transformative process. Internalisation means that the novice has processed the knowledge that was co-constructed with the expert and has made it his or her own unique resource. SCT theorists view knowledge (including language knowledge) not as an object to be possessed or accumulated by the individual (see Sfard, 1998), but an understanding that is 'recreated, modified, and extended in and through collaborative knowledge building and individual understanding' (Wells, 1999: 89).

SCT also presents an alternative perspective on what is considered evidence of cognitive development. The novice's ability to deploy internalised ways of knowing in independent activity is one source of evidence (Lantolf, 2005). Another is the novice's increasing ability to form abstract representations of knowledge. SCT explains this notion of development by reference to different forms of regulation. The novice transforms from being object-regulated (reliant on assistance from concrete physical representations) to other-regulated (reliant on assistance from an expert) to finally becoming self-regulated (independent). Self-regulation means that the novice can construct an abstract mental representation of what was once physically (acoustic or visual) present in external form (Lantolf, 2005). For example, in the case of arithmetic calculations, cognitive development is evident when the novice can add or subtract numbers without the aid of fingers (physical representation), or assistance from a parent or teacher, but by using an abstract representation of numbers.

Thus for Vygotsky (1978, 1987), human cognitive development is a dialectical process, whereby biologically endowed mental capacities are reorganised into uniquely human psychological systems in linguistically mediated interaction. The theory, and research informed by this theory, focus very much on the human dimensions of interaction rather than on the cognitive processes that take place inside the human brain.

Thus any discussion of cognitive development, including L2 development, informed by SCT focuses on the nature of assistance that the expert offers to the novice during interaction. Feedback, including written CF, constitutes a form of assistance. A discussion of written CF from a sociocultural perspective looks carefully at the traits of the feedback and whether it represents appropriate forms of assistance. SCT also highlights the important role that mediational tools play in interaction. These tools enable interaction to take place (e.g. language) but a change of tools (e.g. using computers) may impact on the nature of the assistance provided and the response to the assistance. Thus any discussion of written CF must also take into consideration how it is delivered and how learners engage with it. Finally, and in line with a primary focus on human interaction, SCT considers what drives and influences human behaviour; that is, what individual and context-related variables can explain human behaviour. We noted in Chapter 2 that cognitive theories are now also paying increasing attention to these variables (e.g. motivation, educational context) when explaining learners' response to written CF. However, what distinguishes SCT and AT is that these individual and context-related variables are viewed as a whole system, rather than as a loose set of variables.

In the following sections we focus on some of the key constructs in SCT mentioned briefly in the overview. Although the theory has a number of important and complex constructs, we have selected only those constructs that are of pertinence to explaining L2 development and the role of written CF in this development.

4.2   Key Constructs in SCT

In this section we discuss some of the key constructs in SCT. We explain these theoretical constructs with reference to L2 development, before discussing how they relate more specifically to feedback, including written CF. Our discussion draws heavily on the work of Lantolf and colleagues (Lantolf, 2000a, 2000b; Lantolf & Thorne, 2006) as well as Swain and colleagues (e.g. Swain, 2006a; Swain *et al.*, 2011), whose writings have expanded and explicated these constructs and illustrated how they apply to the field of second language learning. These key constructs are:

(1)   The Zone of Proximal Development (ZPD) and scaffolding;
(2)   Mediation and tools;
(3)   The notion of activity.

4.2.1   The Zone of Proximal Development (ZPD) and scaffolding

As noted above, from a SCT perspective, development occurs in interaction between an expert and a novice. However, one of the implicit assumptions in SCT is that the pairing of an expert and a novice will guarantee that the expert will provide appropriate assistance to the novice. As Lantolf and Thorne (2006: 264) point out, not all forms of assistance are effective and supportive of development. For example, too much assistance can inhibit development (see subsequent discussion). A few important and interrelated characteristics distinguish effective assistance.

The first characteristic is that the assistance needs to enable the novice to perform beyond their current capacities. Thus effective assistance needs to take into consideration the novice's actual level of development and their potential level. The difference between these two levels is referred to as the Zone of Proximal Development (ZPD). Vygotsky's much quoted definition of ZPD refers to the zone as:

> The distance between the actual developmental level as determined by independent problem solving and the level of potential development as determined through problem solving under adult guidance or in collaboration with more capable peers. (Vygotsky, 1978: 86)

To Vygotsky (1978), it was not what the novice can do unassisted but what the novice can achieve with the assistance from others that was of importance for cognitive development. He argued that the novice's ability to take advantage of the assistance offered is more indicative of potential development than the novice's actual performance. According to Vygotsky, a novice who can take advantage of assistance is more likely to show a more rapid rate of development than a novice who cannot take advantage of the assistance offered.

Although the term 'distance' is used in Vygotsky's original definition to refer to the difference between the two levels, actual and potential, a number of researchers (e.g. Lantolf & Poehner, 2014; Swain *et al.*, 2011) reject equating ZPD with the notion of a distance or with a property of an individual. Rather they conceptualise ZPD as a co-constructed activity. This conceptualisation of ZPD draws attention to the negotiated nature of assistance that leads to the development of new capacities.

A number of approaches to assessment draw on the importance of assistance offered to the learner. These include Mediated Learning Experience (MLE) developed by Feuerstein and his colleagues (see Feuerstein *et al.*, 1979; Feuerstein *et al.*, 1988) and dynamic assessment (DA) (see Lantolf & Poehner, 2014; Poehner, 2009; Poehner & Lantolf, 2010 for a discussion of DA in the field of SLA). In MLE and DA, unlike traditional forms of assessment, cooperation between the assessor and the learner is encouraged, as the goal is to provide the type of assistance that will ultimately enable the learner to perform beyond their current level of performance.

For assistance within the ZPD to be effective it needs to have three key traits: it needs to be graduated, contingent and dialogic (Aljaafreh & Lantolf, 1994). Graduated assistance means assistance that is at the minimum level necessary for the novice to complete a task. Too much assistance or not enough assistance is considered detrimental to development. Graduated assistance is negotiated during interaction between the expert and novice in a joint activity with the aim of providing assistance that will encourage the novice to function at his or her potential level of ability.

During interaction, the learner's needs for assistance may change. Thus effective assistance needs to be contingent and dynamic. It should be calibrated to and guided by the evolving needs of the learner rather than provided in a linear, lock-step manner. It needs to be offered when it is needed, withdrawn when there are signs that it is no longer needed because the learner can function independently, and be reintroduced if needed. Van Lier (1996, 2000) noted that effective assistance includes a desire for an ultimate 'handover'. The expert needs to be willing to relinquish control to the novice at the appropriate time.

Therefore, throughout task performance, the expert should provide assistance that is not simply aimed at helping the learner complete the task at hand, but that encourages the learner to take an increasingly greater responsibility for the activity. This assistance should ultimately lead to self-regulated (autonomous) performance, no longer reliant on expert support.

What these characteristics of effective assistance suggest is that assistance within the learner's ZPD cannot be pre-determined. Rather it is 'an act of negotiated discovery' (Lantolf & Aljaafreh, 1995: 620). It involves a process of continuous assessment of what the learner is able to achieve with and without assistance and thus tailoring the assistance accordingly. Furthermore, it implies that the learner also plays an active role. The learner's response to the assistance provides the expert with important cues. It provides the expert with an indication of the learner's ability to take advantage of the assistance offered and hence level of development. Thus at its core this process is dialogic (Wells, 1999). It is continuously adjusted so that the assistance provided is tailored to the learner's evolving needs. Rogoff (1990) used the term 'guided participation' to suggest that both expert guidance and novice participation are essential for effective assistance within the ZPD.

The metaphor that has been used in the literature to describe this finely tuned dynamic assistance is **scaffolding**, a term first introduced by Wood *et al.* (1976) to describe child-adult (tutor) interaction. The authors identified six functions of scaffolding including recruiting interest in the task, marking differences between the learner's solutions and the correct one, and controlling frustrations. The metaphor has been criticised by a number of scholars (see Granott, 2005) particularly for its focus on the adult role, the asymmetry denoted in its definition, and the assumption that the child will choose to use the assistance offered. However, despite these criticisms, it has survived and has spawned many studies.

The power of the metaphor of scaffolding is in its concrete, familiar, visual image. Wilson and Devereux (2014) suggest that the metaphor conjures up the idea of learning as a building under construction. The scaffold is vital for the construction to take place, but as the construction progresses, the scaffold is gradually dismantled and eventually removed. In the case of learning, scaffolding enables the learner to perform a task beyond their current capacity. The scaffolding is dismantled commensurately with the learner's increasing expertise. It can be completely removed when the learner internalises the knowledge co-constructed during the interaction and is able to perform the task independently.

Thus scaffolding is best viewed as a collaborative dialogic activity, co-constructed by the expert and novice. Whereas some scholars (e.g. Weissberg, 2006; Wells, 1998) adopt a narrow definition of scaffolding, confining it only to expert/novice interactions, others employ it to describe an activity involving a group of novices. Granott (2005: 144), for example, redefines scaffolding as the temporary assistance occurring in an ensemble. The ensemble can consist of any number of members. Scaffolding enables the ensemble to perform beyond the levels of any one ensemble member.

In studies of second language learning, a number of researchers (e.g. Donato, 1994; Ohta, 2001; Storch, 2002) have shown that successful scaffolding can occur in small groups and pair work of learners with a similar level of L2 proficiency, and thus no identifiable expert. Some studies (e.g. Ohta, 2001) reported that the role of the expert in such homogenous groups was fluid, with learners taking this role in turn. Fluidity in expert/ novice roles is perhaps not surprising, particularly among adult learners who bring with them a range of perspectives, experiences, and levels of linguistic expertise (van Lier, 1996). Other researchers (e.g. Donato, 1994; Storch, 2002) found evidence of collective scaffolding, where the learners pooled their partial knowledge of the L2. In these instances of co-construction, expertise emerges as a feature of the group/pair rather than any one individual. However, such collective scaffolding was found mainly in small groups and pairs that collaborated; that is, where they functioned as a collective. Furthermore, a novice can self-scaffold, by using, for example, self-directed (private) speech. Private speech enables a novice to gain control of their thinking, of their ability to remember, to pay attention, plan, evaluate and learn (Vygotsky, 1987) (see discussion in Section 4.2.2).

Despite the widespread use of the concept of scaffolding (and perhaps misuse, according to Weissberg, 2006), effective scaffolding is not easily measured. Its distinguishing characteristics that make it a dynamic, fluid, and an interactive system also mean that it is difficult to capture and analyse. Any evaluation of scaffolding requires analysis across time, and involves comparing the performance of the novice before and after assistance has been provided and the nature of the assistance provided.

4.2.1.1   Applying the metaphors of scaffolding and ZPD to written CF

Feedback is a form of assistance. Thus applying the metaphors of scaffolding and ZPD to written CF (provided by the teacher or peer) highlights the need to consider the quality of scaffolding provided in the written CF; that is, whether it displays the key characteristics of effective assistance outlined above: whether it is graduated, contingent and dialogic.

From a SCT perspective, there is no single or pre-determined type of written CF (direct vs. indirect) that is best for learning. Rather, for CF to be effective, it needs to be attuned to the learner's ZPD, taking into consideration the learner's current and potential level of performance (with assistance). If the writing of two learners shows the same linguistic error, the learner who can self-correct their error with just minimal, indirect assistance (e.g. underlining of the error), is viewed as being developmentally more advanced than the learner who requires more direct assistance (e.g. reformulation of the incorrect form). Thus, what may be suitable written CF for one learner may not be suitable for another because effective written CF needs to consider the learner's ability to engage with and make use of the feedback provided. There may also be different ZPDs for different language structures (Aljaafreh & Lantolf, 1994).

Furthermore, the feedback provided needs to be contingently responsive; that is, adjusted in terms of explicitness and specificity in response to the learner's signs of L2 development (see discussion in the following chapter of the scale developed by Aljaafreh & Lantolf, 1994). Rather than viewing corrective feedback as being dichotomous – direct or indirect – SCT views the two forms as lying at two ends of a continuum, and the degree of directness or explicitness varying in response to the learner's evolving needs. Thus, if the learner shows signs of development (the ability to self-correct), the feedback needs to become more indirect. It also suggests that the learner plays an important and active role in the process rather than being merely a passive recipient of feedback.

However, this kind of finely grained written CF, carefully attuned to the specific needs of an individual, may be easier to provide in one-on-one conference sessions. In such contexts, the CF is dialogic and thus more amenable to being graduated and contingent in response to the learner's specific needs as they emerge during the session. In the case of written CF not accompanied by oral interaction, this fine-tuning may be more of a challenge, particularly in educational environments where feedback is given on single drafts. Lee (2014) advocates a process approach to writing instruction, with multiple drafts, so that the feedback provided takes into account the students' evolving needs and abilities over time. Multiple drafts also provide students with opportunities to reflect and respond to feedback. Aljaafreh and Lantolf (1994) suggested the use of portfolio assessment and dialogic journals (see an example of a dialogue journal in Nassaji & Cumming, 2000). In the same vein, Storch and Tapper (1996) advocated a system of student annotations, where students note the main concerns they have about their written texts or their use of specific linguistic structures. These annotations provide the teacher with the student's perspectives about their needs and can guide the teacher when providing feedback. Another way to address this challenge is to offer computer-mediated written CF. Borrowing from the work on DA (see Poehner & Lantolf, 2010), a pre-determined scale ranging from implicit to explicit written CF on the use of targeted structures can be provided in a computerised format. Such a scale has the advantage of efficiency, and can be offered to large cohorts of learners, but its disadvantage is that it cannot be as reactive to the specific needs of the learner as these needs emerge during individual dialogic assistance.

A related point to our discussion of effective written CF is what constitutes evidence of language development following written CF. From a cognitive perspective, what we tend to focus on is the final independent performance. Thus, in research on written CF, evidence of learning following the provision of feedback is reflected in improved accuracy on new pieces of writing or in the more correct use of certain linguistic structures targeted by the feedback (i.e. a focus on the product). From a SCT perspective, using newly gained knowledge in new contexts is one sign of development, but not the only sign of development. If indeed it is taken as the only sign, it may not fully capture a learner's progress. Rather, development can also be seen as a function of the frequency and quality of the assistance required and the learner's responsiveness to the assistance given. Even if the learner's linguistic performance does not become more accurate with respect to the use of certain targeted structures over time, but the type of written CF the learner requires in order to identify and to self-correct an error in the targeted structure becomes less direct, this change reflects L2 development. This greater ability to self-correct, and to even question or reject the feedback given by others (Villamil & Guerrero, 2006) implies a gradual movement from other-regulation to self-regulation. This change can be observed in one pedagogical event (e.g. during a teacher/ student conference) or more realistically over time (successive drafts or different assignments). Development is dynamic. It entails progress as well as some regression in the kind of assistance needed (Lantolf & Aljaafreh, 1995). Hence longitudinal studies may be better to capture development.

4.2.2   Mediation and tools

According to Lantolf (2000b), a distinguishing feature of sociocultural theory is the central role it attributes to mediation. Swain *et al.* (2011: 151) define mediation as a 'process which connects the social and the individual'. Mediation can be achieved via physical or via symbolic tools. Physical or material tools are man-made artefacts (e.g. abacus, calculator, computer) that enable actions (e.g. complex calculations) to take place. Symbolic or social-semiotic tools include, for example, mathematical formulae, musical notes and language. Tools not only enable actions to take place, they also shape the action. Tools also change over time, and as they do they may change the nature of the action. For example, the use of a calculator rather than an abacus shapes the way we perform arithmetic calculations; the limited number of characters allowed when we communicate using Twitter shapes how we conceptualise our experiences.

Of all symbolic tools, language is considered the primary though not exclusive mediational tool (Lantolf & Thorne, 2006). Language mediates interaction between humans. It enables the novice and expert to communicate and coordinate their action (Wells, 1999). For example, language provides speakers with a range of linguistic forms (e.g. Ok, let's see, oh) that can be used to invoke and share attention. It can also be used by the expert and novice to co-construct the scaffold, or by peers to form a collective scaffold (Donato, 1994; Storch, 2002). Within the individual, language also plays a very important role. Language (and other semiotic tools) facilitates the formation of ideas. As Vygotsky (1986: 218) put it: 'Thought is not merely expressed in words; it comes into existence through them.' Language also enables high-level cognitive processes, including self-regulation. Self-directed language (private speech) enables humans to plan their responses rather than react automatically to stimulation from the environment, as is the case with other species. More recent research has also shown that language enables the individual to engage in self-scaffolding, in verbal strategies such as self-directed questions and self explanations in order to resolve language or text related problems (e.g. Knouzi *et al.*, 2010; Negueruela, 2008; Suzuki, 2012; Swain *et al.*, 2011; Watanabe, 2014). Watanabe (2014) also found that learners used language for affective functions such as controlling frustration when confronting a difficult language task.

Swain (2006a) proposed the term **languaging** to describe how language functions to mediate the thinking processes between individuals (collaborative talk) and within the individual (private speech). She defined languaging as a 'process of making meaning and shaping knowledge and experience through language' (2006: 98). She also notes that languaging can take the form of speaking or writing (see also Suzuki, 2012). The act of using language to mediate thinking (i.e. languaging) enables learners to think through solutions to problems they encounter. It transforms thoughts into artefacts which are then available for further contemplation. It also enables learners to gain new insights or a deeper understanding of complex phenomena (Swain *et al.*, 2011). A number of studies have shown a positive relation between the quantity of languaging and language learning gains (e.g. Knouzi *et al.*, 2010; Suzuki, 2012; Swain, 2006a, 2010).

It is important to remember that second language learners have access to two (or more) languages when they language: their L1 and the L2. A number of researchers (e.g. Guerrero & Villamil, 2000; Storch & Aldosari, 2010; Swain & Lapkin, 1998) have documented learners' use of their L1 as a tool to complete language tasks when working in pairs. They found evidence of L1 being used by the learners to mediate task performance, for example, to access L2 words, determine the meaning of these words once accessed, and consider alternative words. Other researchers have investigated how learners use their L1 and L2 to mediate their self-directed speech (thinking), showing that proficiency in the L2 may influence which language is used in private speech, and that using the L1 may in fact result in more successful problem solving (e.g. Centeno-Cortés & Jiménez-Jiménez, 2004).

4.2.2.1   Applying notions of mediation and tools to written CF

Given the centrality of mediation and the role of tools in language development, we need to consider the impact that these tools have on the practice of providing written CF as well as on the processing of the feedback. As mentioned above, tools can be material or symbolic and they not only enable actions to take place, they also shape actions. In relation to written CF, what seems most pertinent is the impact of physical tools, such as computers, and symbolic tools, such as language, on the provision and processing of written CF.

In recent years we have witnessed rapid developments in educational technology, and in the means available to provide and deliver teacher and peer feedback. A vast array of options is available as an alternative to the traditional pen and paper and/or oral face-to-face means of providing written CF (see Ware & Warschauer, 2006). These options include various computer-facilitated means of providing feedback comments, such as Microsoft Word editing functions (e.g. track changes and insert comments), and web-based commenting software that enable teachers to insert pre-written or edited comments and symbols (e.g. Mark My Words, see Milton, 2006). There are also delayed or asynchronous (e.g. email, Discussion Board) and real-time synchronous (e.g. Moos) means of communicating about the feedback provided.

These new means of providing written CF are likely to impact on the practice of providing the feedback in terms of the quantity, quality and nature of the feedback comments. The ease of using pre-written comments may increase the quantity of feedback comments, but at the same time may make these comments less personalised. The new tools may also impact on learners' engagement with written CF. They enable learners to seek further help more easily; to request clarification during deliberations about the feedback received. However, the existing body of research (discussed in the next chapter) suggests that computer-mediated delivery of written CF discourages deep engagement with the feedback.

Engagement with feedback and deliberations about the feedback provided are forms of self-directed speech. When deliberating about the feedback received, the learner may gain perhaps a greater understanding of linguistic conventions or of appropriate word choices, and ultimately internalise the feedback. Internalisation transforms the feedback provided into a resource the learner can use in new pieces of writing. Such deliberations are more likely to occur when learners are asked to revise their text in response to the feedback, to discuss the feedback with their teachers or peers, or to engage in written reflections. The advantage of students working with peers when processing written CF is that learners' deliberations (self-directed speech) become vocalised and thus can elicit further assistance.

4.2.3   The notion of activity: Activity theory

The notion of activity was discussed by Vygotsky, but it was developed into a fully fledged theory, entitled activity theory (AT), only later by scholars such as Leontiev and Engeström. Activity theory focuses investigation on activity rather than on an individual – hence its name. The underlying premise of the theory is that all human activity typically involves other people and mediational tools. Thus, in order to understand what is going on in a particular situation, we need to consider the behaviour of all actors involved in that particular situation and the role of the mediational tools. In this sense, activity theory unifies many of the key constructs in SCT.

The theory has undergone a number of revisions. Each revision has made the theory more complex but also more comprehensive, by including additional elements that may impinge on an activity. The first version of the theory is associated with Vygotsky (1978); the second builds on the work of Leontiev (1979, 1981), a colleague of Vygotsky; and the third was proposed by Engeström (1987, 2001), a Finnish researcher. Engeström's models of AT have received the most prominence in the Western literature and have been applied to a diverse range of learning (e.g. Hardman, 2008) and professional contexts (e.g. Engeström, 2001). These models can be used to describe and analyse a situation, but the ultimate aim of AT is to affect change: to transform and improve the situation investigated (Thorne, 2004).

The initial version of AT is associated with the work of Vygotsky (1978), who attempted to explain the connection between a stimulus and a response, and the central role played by mediational tools. The mediated act, as depicted by a basic triangle in Figure 4.1, has three constituents: **subject, tools** and **object**. The **subject** (person) initiates an action in response to a stimulus. The action is mediated by **tools** and is undertaken to achieve a particular **object.** The tools are placed at the vortex of the triangle because they both enable and constrain activity. The following example may illustrate how this model can be applied to an educational setting.

In a language class, the activity of learning involves the subject (language learner), who initiates an action such as writing a text in response to a teacher's request (stimulus). The action of writing is mediated by physical tools (pen and paper or computer keyboard) and by symbolic tools (the L2). The object of the activity may be to complete the writing task for assessment purposes or for practice in L2 writing. The tools used enable the writing to take place but at the same time constrain the activity. For example, the use of physical tools such as pen and paper constrain the ease of altering or adding ideas to the already written text. Proficiency in the L2 (the symbolic tool) may shape how the learner approaches the writing task.

This relatively simple model is referred to as the first generation (G_1) AT (Engeström, 2001) although it should be noted that Vygotsky himself did not use this nomenclature. The model depicting the mediated act is nevertheless regarded as the theoretical source for later versions of the theory.

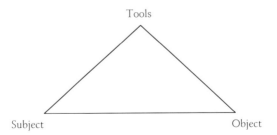

Figure 4.1 Vygotsky's model of a mediated act

The second generation of the theory is associated with the work of Leontiev (1978, 1981) and was an attempt to present the relationship between the individual and the sociocultural setting of an activity more explicitly. Leontiev identified three interrelated hierarchical levels in an activity: (a) **activity** which is driven by an **object-orientated motive**, (b) **actions** which are **goal** directed; and (c) **operations** which respond to immediate **conditions** (Lantolf & Thorne, 2006). Figure 4.2 illustrates this hierarchical three-tiered model.

According to Leontiev (1981), all human purposeful **activity** is directed at an **object**. The activity arises in response to needs or desires. Humans, unlike animals, have both biological (e.g. hunger) and psychological (e.g. learn a second language) needs, the latter having distant rather than immediate consequences. The **motive** is the drive to fulfil needs; it is the impetus that guides human activity towards a specific **object** (e.g. obtain food). Thus motives and objects are closely interrelated, and this may explain why they are represented in the model as one construct. Motives/objects can be instantiated by a range of actions. **Actions** are socioculturally accepted means of fulfilling needs or desires (e.g. hunting or shopping to satisfy hunger; attending formal language classes or using an on-line language teaching course to satisfy the desire to learn a second language) and **goals** are the desired end points of an action. Goals in this sense are attached to specific actions, are conscious and intentional (Wells, 1999), whereas motives may be unconscious. Actions are constrained by the **conditions** of a particular context; that is, the available resources as well as the expected norms. **Operations** are the automatised moves or routines we use to carry out certain actions. Because operations are automatised, they involve no conscious deliberation.

Lantolf and Thorne (2006: 217) draw on Bodker (1997) to suggest that another way of looking at these three levels of activity is as three different analytical perspectives. A schematic representation of the hierarchy is reproduced in the table below (Table 4.1). This way of looking at AT illustrates perhaps more clearly how the theory can be operationalised. Each level of an activity is seen as addressing a different question, and involves a different unit of analysis, participants, and time frame.

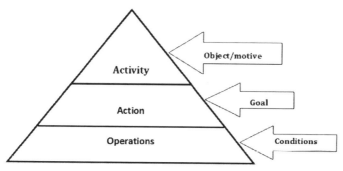

Figure 4.2 Leontiev's activity theory

Table 4.1 Analytical representation of AT (adapted from Lantolf & Thorne, 2006)

Question addressed	Unit of analysis	Orientation	Participants	Time frame
Why	Activity	Motive	Community and/or society	Recurrent
What	Action	Goal	Individual or group	Finite
How	Operation	Condition(s)	Individual	Present moment

Engeström's (1987, 2001) second generation (G_2) AT expanded on Leontiev's work. This version (see Figure 4.3) excludes explicit reference to actions and goals but includes mediational means. The uppermost sub-triangle of Figure 4.3 represents individual and group actions embedded in a collective activity system. As in previous models, the subject is the individual or group; the object is the orientation of that activity, which is moulded into outcomes with the help of tools. The tools used are mediating artefacts (symbolic or material) that enable the activity to take place.

What distinguishes this version of AT is that it elaborates on operations and conditions present within the broader context. It views all activities as taking place within a broader context of a **community** (real or imagined) with its historical, institutional and local rules and division of labour. The **rules** are the norms and conventions of the community or within an institution (e.g. turn-taking rules in a classroom). **Division of labour** refers to the hierarchy in the community, and the power relationships between the subjects within the community (e.g. teacher and students). The use of double-headed arrows within the model reflects that all aspects of the activity shape and are shaped by each other. An example many teachers working in ESL classes are familiar with is the rules of behaviour regarding how students address the teacher. Students come into the ESL class with their own notions of what is the appropriate way to address their teacher, notions which were shaped by their previous educational experiences. Initially they may be reluctant to adopt new, perhaps less formal forms of address (e.g. using their teacher's first name). However over time, a new set of rules may emerge. These revised rules are influenced by and in turn may influence the division of labour (hierarchical relationship in the class) and the mediational means (i.e. the form of address).

Thus analysis informed by this second generation AT enables researchers to focus on the interaction of multiple individuals and social forces simultaneously. Such an analysis takes into consideration all the participants in the activity and recognises that each participant comes into an activity with their own social history. This social history will shape how each participant views and interprets actions and events. This notion of human intentionality, shaped by previous experiences, is captured by the term **agency.**

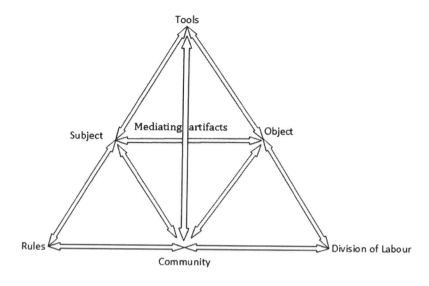

Figure 4.3 Activity Theory, G_2 (adapted from Engeström, 2001)

Agency is the capacity to establish personal goals and choose the means to achieve those goals (Lantolf & Pavlenko, 2001). This may explain, in part, variations in individual behaviour within any one activity because the same activity can be realised through different actions and different mediational means (see Coughlan & Duff, 1994). It also means that even though overt learner behaviour may appear the same, the activity underway may be very different. Individuals' actions may be orientated towards achieving different goals, and thus assigned different levels of significance. Furthermore these goals are dynamic and can change during the life of the activity (Lantolf & Appel, 1994).

Engeström's (2001) third generation (G_3) AT is one of multiple interacting activity systems. This version attempts to show that any activity takes place in a community of multiple perspectives/voices. For example, if we consider two interacting systems (see Figure 4.4), then we have a co-constructed shared object arising from two interrelated activity systems. In a sense, this co-constructed object alludes to the notion of **intersubjectivity**, a term coined by Rommetveit (1985). Rommetveit defined it a state where the participants come to share a common perspective and an equal commitment to the task. In order to attain intersubjectivity, participants need to suspend (perhaps temporarily) their own perspective in order to accommodate the perspectives of others in the activity. According to Wertsch (1991), coming to value another person's perspective may enable the individual to better understand and even critique one's own perspective.

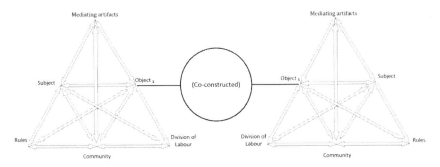

Figure 4.4 Activity theory G_3: Two interacting activity systems (adapted from Engeström, 2001)

In summary, from an AT perspective, what humans do to satisfy physical and psychological needs is seen as a socially mediated action rather than an individual action occurring in a social context (Swain *et al.*, 2011). Thus AT provides a framework that can be used to analyse various aspects of observable human behaviour simultaneously, moving away from compartmentalised types of analyses, which consider only one learner or one set of context factors in isolation (e.g. macro and micro factors discussed in Chapter 2). AT theorises context and thus helps make visible the relationship between the individual, the mediating tools, and the social context in which the activity takes place. It also makes it clear that we cannot predict or pre-determine what humans will do. For example, teachers cannot predict what students will or will not learn, or whether students will engage in a task (e.g. respond to written CF in a pre-determined way). As Lantolf (2005) points out, researchers and teachers can try to engage learners in activities that promote learning, but they cannot guarantee that learning will take place. Similarly, although the context determines which linguistic forms learners are exposed to (via instruction and/or targeted by the written CF) and which forms are deemed significant (see research by Norton & Toohey, 2001; Peirce, 1995), within these contextual constraints, it is the individual and the meaning and significance that the individual assigns to various activities in the learning situation that will determine which structures will be mastered.

Finally it should be noted that what perhaps has not received sufficient attention in all models of activity is the emotional dimension of the individual. Swain (2013) argues that the impact of emotions on human activity and cognitive development has been largely ignored in research on language learning. Benesch (2012) makes a similar argument regarding the neglect of emotions in the literature on language teaching. These emotions include enjoyment, admiration, pride, dislike, shame and boredom, and may be intricately linked to notions of learner identity. Swain (personal communication, October 2014) points out that although in the original definition of scaffolding Wood *et al.* (1976) noted that one of the functions of scaffolding is to control feelings of frustration, this emotional aspect is not mentioned in most discussions and research on scaffolding and ZPD. The reasons why emotions have been largely ignored are perhaps because they are difficult to define, and to measure (Imai, 2010), and it is difficult to predict their impact on learning. Nevertheless, emotions may explain learners' (and teachers') goals and actions in an activity. Furthermore, in interactions, it is the emotions of all participants and their alignment that need to be considered (see Storch, 2004, 2013).

4.2.3.1   *Applying AT to written CF*

From an AT perspective, written CF is viewed more broadly; that is, not just as a stand-alone occurrence of the provision of assistance but as an activity. This activity takes place in a specific educational context and not, as Ortega (2012) correctly points out, in a social vacuum. AT provides us with an analytical framework to map, analyse, and interpret the activity of written CF. In order to understand this activity we need to consider the context-specific dimensions of feedback (Lee, 2014), the participants' (teachers and students) orientation to the activity (object) and the goals that their actions attempt to achieve. We can employ either the second (G_2) or third generation (G_3) of AT. To analyse and interpret the behaviour of teachers (type of feedback comments provided) or of learners (e.g. response to feedback comments from teachers or peers) then G_2 of AT could be employed. To consider the interaction of a learner and teacher activities or of a small group of learners in a peer-response activity, then G_3 of AT would be a more suitable analytical framework. This framework takes into consideration the nature of the shared object arising from the interacting activity systems, and can help explain occasions when this shared object is not attained (see Lee & Schallert, 2008, discussed in the next chapter).

Operationalizing AT in the L2 writing classroom and the terms used, the participants (teachers, learners) are the **subjects** whose **actions** (e.g. composing texts, providing feedback, reacting to the feedback) are mediated by symbolic (the language used in written or oral feedback comments) or material **tools** (e.g. computer programs) that are used to deliver the feedback. The **community** is the classroom or educational programme within which the activity takes place. This community may have **rules** that determine what is the appropriate form of written CF: the nature, the mode and frequency of written CF provision. These rules may determine, for example, whether the feedback provided is direct (e.g. reformulations) or indirect (e.g. underlining the error), whether it is given on interim or only on final drafts, in written or computer-mediated form (tools), whether it is comprehensive or targeted feedback, and if targeted, which linguistic forms are targeted. The **division of labour** relates to the status of teachers vis-à-vis other stakeholders in the educational institution, or the status of certain peers in a peer-response activity. For example, in certain educational institutions, the kind of written feedback that the teacher provides is not an autonomous teacher decision, but one mandated by the institutional policies. However, rules and division of labour may be shaped not only by the immediate local context but also by government educational policies, by society at large, and by historical and cultural factors, all of which influence beliefs and shape policies. These factors shape, for example, beliefs concerning the importance of accuracy, what are considered 'good teaching practices' (see Sullivan, 2000), and appropriate forms of written CF (Al Shahrani & Storch, 2014; Lee, 2014). The analysis can also identify existing tensions that may exist in the system, tensions that may be due to conflicting beliefs of the various stakeholders in the community. Exposing these tensions may help in identifying how we can resolve these tensions and the kind of innovations that can be implemented in the provision of feedback (Thorne, 2004).

The **subjects** (teachers and students) in the activity are driven by certain motives (**objects**), and their actions are orientated to achieve certain **goals.** Humans, as active **agents**, have the capacity to establish goals and to choose the means to achieve their goals. Learners' goals are shaped by a host of affective factors: previous language learning experiences, language learning beliefs as well as attitudes towards writing and accuracy (see for example Rummel's (2014) study discussed in Chapter 3). Their actions are also shaped by the broader context in which writing and the written CF activity take place.

Using van Lier's (2000) notion of affordances, written CF can be perceived as an affordance, an opportunity for learning, but only if it triggers further action. Written CF affords learners the opportunity to learn but will not guarantee learning unless the learner perceives these linguistic affordances as valuable and acts on them. Learners, and particularly adult learners, are individuals who may choose not only whether to consider the feedback but also whether to accept or to reject some of the feedback provided by the expert. This may explain why some learners pay close attention to written CF, whereas others fail to do so. The focus on human intentionality within a particular context can explain why written CF may be incorporated in revised texts but why ultimately it may or may not lead to L2 development.

As discussed in Chapter 3, research informed by cognitive perspectives has until recently tended to focus largely on factors affecting cognitive processes such as the noticing of the feedback, and how certain traits of the feedback (e.g. direct/indirect, grammatical structures targeted) may impact on these processes. More recently this research has begun to consider how individual learner factors (e.g. language learning aptitude, motivational intensity) as well as context-related factors may impact on these cognitive processes. In contrast, SCT eschews discussion of cognition. There is no reference, for example, to short-term memory capacity or the nature of noticing. Instead, SCT focuses on social processes (interaction) and AT focuses mainly on learner and context-related factors. This is because these theories view learners as active agents who assign relevance and significance to certain actions. When receiving written CF, learners exercise volitional control over what they notice in the feedback and the action they take in response to the feedback they receive. Lantolf and Pavlenko (2001: 145) remind us that learners 'need to be understood as people, which in turn means we need to appreciate their human agency. As agents, learners actively engage in constructing the terms and conditions of their learning.'

Similarly, in the case of teachers, within the constraints of the institutional rules, teachers vary in their written CF practices. What may appear as random variation in teacher actions may be explained by teachers' goals. Teachers may be attempting to fulfil a number of pedagogical and interpersonal goals in their feedback comments (F. Hyland, 2011; Hyland & Hyland, 2006a; Leki, 1990). In responding to their students' writing, teachers take into consideration not only the errors made but also the student who made the errors (see F. Hyland, 1998; Lee & Schallert, 2008). Leki (1990), for example, reported that teachers may be concerned about achieving conflicting goals. They may be concerned that their feedback on language use could appropriate and silence the student writer's voice because of the inherently asymmetrical teacher/student power relationship. Teachers' goals and views concerning written CF, in turn, may be shaped by their professional knowledge and their own language learning experience.

Another distinguishing feature of research on written CF using AT as a theoretical framework is that it focuses on individuals in the activity and social/institutional factors simultaneously, rather than drawing a distinction between micro and macro factors. From an AT perspective, it is difficult to separate these factors because these factors inevitably interact. As Hyland and Hyland (2006: 86) point out, 'Feedback is not simply a disembodied reference to student text but an interactive part of the whole context of learning.' Thus to gain a better understanding of learner and teacher behaviour with respect to written CF, we need to consider the interaction of individual and context-specific factors. Furthermore, research informed by this theoretical perspective tends to adopt a longitudinal case study design. An analysis of one written CF event can provide a snapshot of the activity; a longitudinal study examining feedback on multiple drafts can provide insights into how the written CF activity may change over time, with possible changes in goals, rules, and accepted norms of behaviour.

4.3   Summary and Conclusions

In summary, SCT justifies the use of written CF for L2 development primarily by seeing feedback as a form of assistance offered by an expert (teacher or peer) to a novice in interaction. The basic premise of SCT, however, is that not all forms of assistance are effective. To be effective and facilitate L2 development, written CF needs to take into consideration the learner's existing and potential stages of cognitive development (ZPD), and be dynamic; that is, the nature of the written CF needs to be carefully attuned to the changing needs of the learner (scaffolded). Language, as a symbolic tool, enables the feedback provider (teacher or peer) to adjust the feedback to the learner's needs. Language also mediates thinking: it enables the learner to deliberate about the feedback, and ultimately to internalise and appropriate it. Other material tools (e.g. computers) may also shape the nature of the feedback provided and how learners engage with the feedback.

Beyond describing the type of effective written CF and how tools mediate the delivery and processing of feedback, employing SCT and AT can help to answer the perennial question of *why*. Analysis from an AT perspective can shed light on *why* teachers adopt certain written CF practices, *why* students respond in a particular way to the feedback they receive, *why* written CF leads to L2 learning for some students but not for others. According to AT, whether the learner engages and retains the written CF provided may depend not only on the nature of the feedback but also on the individual learner's orientation to the feedback activity, the goals the learner desires to achieve, as well as the cultural, institutional and social dimensions within the broader context in which the written CF activity takes place.

Finally, it is also important to remember that SCT provides a different way of viewing and assessing L2 development, following the provision of written CF. Development from this perspective is viewed not only in terms of improved accuracy in subsequent texts but also in terms of increasing self-regulation. If the learner can correct their errors by being provided with an implicit clue (e.g. indication in the margin that there is an error in a particular line), whereas previously that learner needed more explicit clues (e.g. using error codes), this is also taken as evidence of the learner's L2 development. The next chapter reviews studies which have investigated written CF and that have been informed by SCT and/or AT.

5 Socioculturally Informed Research on Written CF for L2 Development

5.0   Introduction

In Chapter 4 we discussed the main tenets of SCT and how the theory views cognitive development, including L2 learning, and the importance it attributes to effective assistance and thus by implications to written CF, a form of assistance. The theory highlights the importance of tools, both symbolic and material, which mediate all human cognitive development. We then considered AT, a theory originating in the writing of Vygotsky, and which views written CF as an activity with interacting social and psychological dimensions. We also noted that research informed by SCT employs alternative approaches to research design and to what constitutes evidence of L2 development.

In this chapter we critically review studies on written CF informed by SCT and AT. This feedback may be provided by teachers or by peers, in written and/or oral forms (conferences), in traditional pen and paper format or electronically via the computer. We note from the outset that this body of research is relatively small. It tends to be longitudinal and interpretative, with multiple sources of qualitative data (e.g. recorded interactions, reflections, observations). Research informed by SCT and AT favours conducting the investigation in situ, in authentic language learning environments (e.g. language classrooms, one-on-one tutorials) and there is no attempt to control that environment. Rather, the investigators attempt to account for the complexities that are inherent in authentic language learning environments. Case study is a commonly used research design, allowing for moment-by-moment (microgenetic) investigation of development or development over time. This approach to research does not mean that quantitative data and analysis are excluded; but rather that quantification does not form the main focus of research and the basis for interpretation of findings.

The discussion in this chapter is segmented into three main sections, mirroring the three main sections in the previous chapter: feedback as a form of scaffolding within the ZPD, the impact of mediational tools on the provision and processing of written CF, and investigations of written CF as an activity. Each section concludes with a summary of the main findings and some indications of future research needs. The chapter then concludes with an overall summary of what empirical research informed by SCT and AT tells us about written CF.

5.1   Feedback as a Form of Scaffolding within the ZPD

As discussed in the previous chapter, from a SCT perspective, written CF is a form of assistance provided to learners. However, for that assistance to be effective, it needs to be co-constructed and dynamic, so that it can be graduated and contingently responsive to the learner's evolving needs. A number of studies have investigated whether the corrective feedback provided to L2 learners on their writing accords with the characteristics of scaffolding, taking into consideration the learners' ZPD. We divide our discussion into two subsections according to the source of the feedback. We begin with feedback provided by teachers and then discuss feedback provided by peers. Where the study involved a novel or complex research design (e.g. Aljaafreh & Lantolf, 1994; Brooks & Swain, 2009; Nassaji, 2012), we provide a detailed description of the study.

5.1.1   Corrective feedback on L2 writing provided by teachers

The study that is most often cited as illustrative of scaffolding in the provision of CF by a tutor is that by Aljaafreh and Lantolf (1994). Although the study looked at the provision of oral rather than written CF on students' L2 writing, we discuss this study here because it is a seminal study. It was the first study to investigate CF on L2 writing using SCT as its theoretical framework and the first to adopt a radically different view of L2 development. Furthermore, Aljaafreh and Lantolf designed a 'regulatory scale' of CF which attempted to operationalise scaffolded CF so that the feedback offered is graduated and contingently responsive to the learner's performance. This scale has since been used by a number of other researchers.

Aljaafreh and Lantolf's (1994) study reported on the use of this regulatory scale of corrective feedback. The study used a longitudinal case study approach, examining the interactions between a tutor and three ESL students in five individual consultations over an eight-week period. Each session dealt with a different composition but targeted four linguistic structures. The procedure adopted was that the tutor read each composition before the consultation but provided no written corrective feedback. Instead, feedback was provided orally and was guided by the regulatory scale of assistance developed by the researchers.

The regulatory scale of assistance has 12 levels (0–12). The nature of the assistance that the tutor provides depends on the learner's response; that is, the feedback begins with implicit strategies, and depending on the learner's response, it becomes more specific and explicit, if necessary. As shown in Figure 5.1, the first level, Level 0, is one where no assistance is provided. In the Aljaafreh and Lantolf study, it involved the tutor asking the learner to re-read their text and in the process self-identify and correct any errors independently before the tutorial session began. Level 1 is labelled the 'collaborative frame', where the mere presence of a tutor signals the potential for collaboration between the expert (tutor) and the novice (language learner). Assistance, at the most implicit level, begins at Level 2. The other end of the scale (Levels 10–12) include the most explicit forms of assistance which involve providing the learner with the correct form, with or without further explanations and examples.

Level	Nature of assistance
0	Tutor asks the learner to read, find the errors, and correct them independently, prior to the tutorial.
1	Construction of a 'collaborative frame' prompted by the presence of the tutor as a potential dialogic partner.
2	Prompted or focused reading of the sentence that contains the error by the learner or the tutor.
3	Tutor indicates that something may be wrong in a segment (e.g. sentence, clause, line – 'Is there anything wrong in this sentence?').
4	Tutor rejects unsuccessful attempts at recognising the error.
5	Tutor narrows down the location of the error (e.g. tutor repeats or points to the specific segment which contains the error).
6	Tutor indicates the nature of the error, but does not identify the error (e.g. 'There is something wrong with the tense marking here').
7	Tutor identifies the error ('You can't use an auxiliary here').
8	Tutor rejects learner's unsuccessful attempts at correcting the error.
9	Tutor provides clues to help the learner arrive at the correct form (e.g. 'It is not really past but some thing that is still going on').
10	Tutor provides the correct form.
11	Tutor provides some explanation for use of the correct form.
12	Tutor provides examples of the correct pattern when other forms of help fail to produce an appropriate responsive action.

Figure 5.1 Regulatory scale-implicit (strategic) to explicit (Aljaafreh & Lantolf, 1994: 471, reproduced with permission)

Aljaafreh and Lantolf used two criteria to assess learners' language development. The first, a more traditional product-orientated criterion, was accurate language use. The researchers examined the learners' use of the targeted linguistic structures in successive compositions for evidence of greater accuracy in the use of these structures. The second, a more radical criterion, took into consideration the level of assistance or regulation required. The researchers used the scale showing different levels of assistance as also denoting different levels of regulations (Figure 5.1). Using this scale, a learner at Level 0 is considered to be on the verge of self-regulation (i.e. independent performance). At Levels 2–3 a learner displays partial self-regulation (ability to self-correct but performance is not automatised). Towards the end of the scale (Levels 10–12), the learner is other-regulated (reliant on the assistance from the tutor). In order to place each learner on the scale, the researchers considered the frequency and quality of the assistance needed in the correction of the targeted errors in the same session (but for subsequent instances of the same error) as well as in subsequent tutorials. Movements along the scale towards self-regulation were taken to represent language development.

Based on detailed analyses of the recorded session protocols and the compositions, the researchers show different trajectories of development for each learner, depending on the grammatical structure targeted and the learner's level of required assistance (level of regulation). For example, in the case of one learner, even though the use of the structure (modal + main verb) in successive compositions did not show greater accuracy, the frequency and type of assistance required became less explicit over time. The researchers argue that this change provides evidence of L2 development as the learner became more self-regulated.

Ellis (2010) suggests that in order to implement such carefully and individually attuned CF, the teacher needs considerable skill. Lantolf and Aljaafreh (1995) admit to the difficulty of adhering to the regulatory scale in finely tuning the assistance provided to the learners. In reviewing the transcripts of the sessions from their earlier (1994) study, they observe that the tutor at times provided more explicit assistance than was necessary. Furthermore, they reported that development was not smooth. There were occasions of backsliding when the learners required more frequent and/or more explicit feedback on the use of the targeted structures compared to previous sessions. Nevertheless, they point out that over time all three ESL learners showed evidence of linguistic development in their ability to use and/or self-correct the targeted structures.

Two subsequent studies set out to investigate empirically whether carefully scaffolded CF is superior to non-scaffolded feedback. The study by Erlam *et al.* (2013) was conducted with adult ESL learners in New Zealand; the study by Nassaji and Swain (2000) with adult ESL learners in

Canada. Both involved providing targeted feedback during oral conferences on writing. It is interesting to note that despite reporting similar findings, the authors of the two studies drew very different conclusions.

Erlam et al.'s (2013) study had two groups of learners participating in two individual oral feedback sessions. One group (n=7) received scaffolded feedback, roughly graduated in terms of explicitness in response to the learners' response to the feedback; the other group (n=8) received explicit corrections. The study found that scaffolded feedback encouraged learners to self-correct but did not lead to a reduction in the assistance needed from one session to the next. In the case of the other group, the learners who received explicit feedback often failed to produce the correct form, despite the feedback. Somewhat puzzling, the researchers concluded that scaffolded feedback may not be effective nor superior to explicit CF. They noted that scaffolded feedback was very time consuming (taking just over 26 minutes on average compared to approximately 10.5 minutes for non-scaffolded feedback), and thus not a very expedient way of providing CF.

However, given some of the problems in the research design, the findings and indeed the conclusions drawn are somewhat problematic. The first problem is that the two groups differed in terms of their L2 proficiency and the English classes they were enrolled in. The students in the group that received scaffolded feedback were of fairly low L2 proficiency (IELTS 3–3.5), and were enrolled in a general English stream; the students in the group that received explicit feedback were deemed of higher L2 proficiency (IELTS levels not disclosed), and were enrolled in an 'Academic English' class where there was a greater emphasis on written English. Thus it may be that this explicit feedback group required shorter feedback treatments (length of time to provide the feedback) because of their higher proficiency and exposure to CF in their language classes. The second problem is the short duration of the study. Whereas the learners in Aljaafreh and Lantolf's (1994) study met the tutor on five occasions, the learners in Erlam et al.'s study attended only two individual conferences. If we accept the claim made by a number of researchers (e.g. Lantolf & Aljaafreh, 1995; Larsen-Freeman, 2006; Verspoor et al., 2008) that regression is a normal part of development, it is difficult to ascertain whether what Erlam et al. observed was evidence of temporary regression rather than lack of development. Longitudinal studies, where learners are provided with feedback on more than one or two occasions, could provide more convincing evidence of a developmental trajectory.

Unlike the studies discussed above (Aljaafreh & Lantolf, 1994; Erlam et al., 2013), Nassaji and Swain's (2000) study used a larger number of measures of language development. These included the nature of assistance the learners required, learners' ability to self-correct in subsequent conferences, and performance on pre- and post-tests. The study investigated whether carefully attuned CF, provided within the learner's ZPD, is more effective than random CF (irrespective of the learner's ZPD).

Nassaji and Swain's (2000) case study involved two adult intermediate ESL learners receiving targeted corrective feedback on the use of English articles. One learner received systematic feedback (the ZPD learner), based on the scale developed by Aljaafreh and Lantolf (1994); the other (non-ZPD) received feedback that did not accord with the scale. The data included four tutor/learner sessions (recorded) and the learners' performance on four cloze tests. The study found that the learner who received feedback attuned to her ZPD was able to self-correct with less explicit feedback as well as to show greater gains in the use of articles on the post-test compared to the non-ZPD learner. Thus the findings confirmed that assistance that is scaffolded and sensitive to the learners' ZPD has a greater impact on learning than randomly provided assistance. The findings also confirmed the need for longitudinal studies in order to assess whether scaffolded feedback results not only in greater self-regulation but also in improved grammatical accuracy.

However, as Nassaji (2012) admits, studies on the impact of scaffolded feedback provided in conferences held outside the language class may not be generalisable to regular classrooms, where such intensive one-on-one sessions are rare. Thus his 2012 study set out to investigate the merits of scaffolded (or negotiated feedback, the term Nassaji used in this study) in a classroom context, using both written and oral CF. The study compared the impact of three types of feedback: negotiated feedback, minimally negotiated feedback, and non-negotiated feedback on the use of articles and prepositions. The participants, adult ESL learners in two intact classes, received three rounds of feedback on their journal writing. In the first round, the teacher provided written reformulations on a selected sample of the targeted structures (i.e. non-negotiated written feedback); in the second round (a week later), the teacher provided oral reformulations when learners failed to provide correct revisions (i.e. minimally negotiated feedback). The third round was similar to the second round, but when a prompt failed to elicit the correct form the teacher negotiated with the student, beginning with the most implicit request, until a successful resolution to the error was reached. Each round was followed by an immediate and delayed post-test which consisted of each learner correcting a set of sentences containing errors in the targeted structures. Nassaji found that negotiated feedback led to greater accuracy on the post-tests than non-negotiated and minimally negotiated feedback, but only for the use of articles. The negotiations enabled the learners to gain a greater understanding of this rule-based structure. This was not the case for the use of prepositions. However, as the author admits, there was no evidence that the feedback led to the learners' ability to use articles accurately in new pieces of writing. Moreover, we need to bear in mind that the improved performance following the third round of feedback may have been due to a cumulative effect, given that feedback on the same structures was given in two previous rounds.

To date, studies investigating CF as a form of scaffolding have mainly considered feedback provided on writing but orally in individual conferences. To some extent this is not surprising, given that for the feedback to be scaffolded – that is, contingently responsive to the learner's performance – it needs to be co-constructed. Such co-construction is more easily implemented via oral dialogue, where the learner's response to the feedback is immediate. Nevertheless, feedback on successive drafts of writing could also be perceived as a form of dialogue and analysed in terms of whether it accords with the characteristics of scaffolding. Written feedback comments on successive drafts can reflect the quality of the scaffold offered in terms of levels of directness. From a SCT perspective, written CF that remains direct regardless of the learners' developing competence constitutes ineffective assistance.

The only studies to date that have investigated written CF on the writing of L2 writers using the construct of scaffolding are by Morton et al. (2014) and Storch (2014), the latter study extending the analysis of the data set used in Morton et al. The studies investigated retrospectively the amount and nature of written feedback, including written CF, provided by a supervisor (Storch) to her MA student on three successive drafts of the student's literature review chapter. Feedback was provided electronically (using Microsoft Word comment functions and symbols) and was followed by an individual conference. All instances of written feedback (comments in the margins, symbols, deletions and reformulations) were counted. They were then analysed for focus (language, content, structure, other) and for degree of explicitness. Explicitness was operationlised on a continuum, with the most explicit feedback (e.g. deletions, directives) at one end of the continuum and the least explicit or implicit forms at the other. Less explicit forms of feedback (e.g. underlining, suggestions) are open to interpretation by the writer. However, the authors acknowledge that this categorisation of feedback for degree of explicitness may not be how the learner interpreted the intent of the feedback comments.

The studies found a decrease in the amount of feedback provided by the supervisor and a shift in focus and explicitness. However, this change in the quantity and nature of feedback was evident only on the third draft. On the first and second draft, there was a substantial amount of feedback given, perhaps due to the ease of providing feedback electronically. However, the supervisor also admitted to a lack of awareness of the amount of feedback she provided (see also Basturkmen et al., 2014). Corrective feedback predominated in line with the findings reported in other studies on supervisors' feedback (e.g. Basturkmen et al., 2014; Bitchener et al., 2010; Kumar & Stracke, 2007). A large proportion of all feedback comments related to content on the first draft, to structure on the second draft, and to language (grammar and expression) on the third draft. This pattern in the focus of the feedback comments aligns with a process approach to writing, where feedback on language use is provided only on later drafts. Feedback on language use continued to be quite explicit (deletions, reformulations) on all three drafts. However, feedback given in the form of comments became less explicit over time. On the third draft, compared to earlier drafts, there were more questions than statements and directives.

The assumption underlying feedback in supervisor-supervisee interaction is that, with the growing expertise of the supervisee over time, the amount of feedback declines and becomes less explicit. Thus the supervisor on reflection wondered whether these findings reflect missed opportunities for reduced scaffolding, and for a handover of responsibility to the student particularly for grammatical accuracy. However, as there was no analysis of the successive texts for accuracy, it is difficult to conclude whether the supervisee required a smaller quantity and less explicit forms of assistance.

5.1.2   Feedback provided by peers

Scaffolded feedback can be provided not only by an expert but also by peers of similar levels of L2 proficiency and linguistic expertise. A series of descriptive studies on classroom peer response activities conducted by Guerrero and Villamil (Guerrero & Villamil, 1994, 2000; Villamil & Guerrero, 1996, 1998) used the notion of regulation to characterise the interactions and the relationships learners formed during such activities. These studies also examined the nature of the feedback provided, particularly in terms of scaffolding. The studies were conducted in Puerto Rico, with 54 intermediate ESL learners working in pairs. Although the learners dealt with different aspects of the written texts, grammar seemed to receive the most attention from the peers (Villamil & Guerrero, 1998). The researchers found that students were able to provide effective assistance using a range of scaffolding strategies such as advising, requesting clarifications and providing mini grammar lessons when needed. There was also evidence of mutual scaffolding (Guerrero & Villamil, 2000). What seemed to facilitate the learners' interactions was the use of the shared L1. Thus the researchers concluded that the peer response activity succeeded in creating an instructional space where learning was encouraged.

In their 1998 paper, the researchers reported on the impact of the peer response activity on L2 writing, focusing on the final drafts of a subsection of their data (the final drafts of 14 learners). The analysis revealed that a very large proportion (74%) of the suggested revisions, relating to both content and grammar, were incorporated in the final drafts. The researchers claimed that this uptake behaviour provides evidence of language development but admitted that such claims are tentative, and that future studies need to include the learners' new writing.

A number of studies have compared the impact of peer and teacher feedback on revisions, reporting that students incorporate more of the teachers' feedback than of their peers' feedback comments (e.g. Connor & Asenavage, 1994; Tsui & Ng, 2000; Yang et al., 2006). However, only two studies have compared the impact of teacher and peer feedback through the lens of sociocultural theory. These studies provide different perspectives on the utility of peer feedback.

Zhao (2010), who compared how much a group of EFL students in China incorporated and understood of teacher and peer written CF, found that although students incorporated a larger proportion of teacher than peer feedback in their revised drafts, they understood a greater proportion of the peer feedback. Drawing on SCT and the notion of internalisation (Lantolf & Thorne, 2006), Zhao argues that understanding is key to the process of internalising the feedback. Zhao's claims accorded with the findings of Brooks and Swain (2009).

Brooks and Swain's (2009) study investigated the impact of different sources of feedback on the learners' final revisions. In this small-scale study (N=4), the learners attended four sessions. In the first session they wrote a text collaboratively, in the second they compared their text to a reformulated version, in the third they participated in a stimulated recall session, and in the final session they revised individually their original, collaboratively written text. Sessions 1, 2 and 3 were audio and video recorded. The researchers treated the individually revised texts as post-tests to investigate which of the three available sources of expertise the learners drew on when revising their original text: the interaction that took place with peers (in Sessions 1 and 2), the reformulated text, the interaction with the researcher herself (Session 3). All recorded talk data was coded for instances of languaging episodes. The learners' original texts were then compared to the revised texts and each revision made was linked to the source of the expertise: peer, reformulation, researcher or to self, the latter referring to revisions that were not discussed in any of the prior sessions.

The study found that the largest number of languaging episodes occurred at the collaborative writing stage, when the learners resolved problems they encountered while composing. Furthermore, the resolutions the learners reached during those episodes were enduring. A very high proportion of the solutions to language problems that the learners discussed and resolved during the collaborative writing session (Session 1) were maintained in the revised texts produced in Session 4.

In contrast, some of the erroneous structures that were reformulated and subsequently discussed with the researcher reappeared in the post-test. One possible explanation offered by the researchers for these findings is that the reformulations and assistance provided by the researcher dealt with structures that were perhaps beyond the learners' developmental stage (ZPD). Peers, on the other hand, provided each other with assistance that was more attuned to their needs and developmental stage. Another possible explanation for these findings is that the assistance peers provided each other during the co-authoring stage was the most dynamic of all sources: it drew on the knowledge of both learners and was contingently responsive to their needs as they arose. The languaging episodes showed evidence of collective scaffolding. Scaffolding was absent in the reformulation feedback and, to some extent, in the interaction with the researcher. The study thus highlights the importance of corrective feedback that is dynamic and responsive to the learners' needs. However, whether revisions made to the text constitute evidence of language learning is contentious. As we stated in Chapter 1, it is performance on new pieces of writing rather than revisions that is taken to constitute evidence of language learning following CF.

To conclude this section, the question we ask ourselves as researchers and teachers is whether scaffolded written CF is indeed more effective than random feedback. The limited body of research on CF as a form of scaffolding within a learner's ZPD suggests that feedback that is carefully attuned to individual learner ability – that is, ability to understand and take advantage of the feedback offered – is more effective than random feedback. Scaffolded CF leads to L2 development, when such development is measured in terms of (a) performance on revised or subsequent texts, (b) performance on post-tests and/or (c) reduced reliance on explicit feedback (including ability to self-correct). Such feedback can be provided by an expert (e.g. tutor) or by L2 peers.

The extant body of research, however, is not only small in number but also small in scale. This is perhaps not surprising given the detailed analysis that such studies entail and the fact that scaffolded CF needs to be tailored to the individual learner's needs. Nevertheless, for stronger claims to be made about the efficacy of scaffolded feedback, more studies are needed in a range of contexts and with different cohorts of students (not just ESL or EFL). Such studies need to be carefully designed and longitudinal to allow for the normal occurrence of regression in the trajectory of language development. They need to include data on levels of regulation over time as well as new writing in order to assess the impact of scaffolded assistance on the learner's writing.

Furthermore, with the exception of the studies discussed above (Morton *et al.*, 2014; Storch, 2014), there have been no other studies to date that have adopted a SCT perspective to investigate the quality of teacher-written feedback comments on successive drafts of students' writing. Weissberg (2006), among others, has called for teachers to critically reflect on their own feedback practices. The widespread use of interim drafts in L2 writing classes, and particularly in graduate pedagogy, provides instructors with the opportunity to do so via retrospective action research, and to examine whether the kind of corrective feedback they provide their students is graduated and responsive to their students' evolving needs.

5.2   Mediation and Use of Tools in the Provision and Processing of Written CF

In this section we review studies that focused on the use of two types of mediational tools: symbolic tools and material tools. In discussing symbolic tools, we consider how language mediates the processing of written CF as learners deliberate about the feedback they receive. In discussing material tools, we consider how the use of computer-mediated modes of providing written CF impacts on the provision of this feedback, and on how learners engage with this electronic form of feedback.

5.2.1   Language as a tool: Oral and written languaging when processing written CF

As noted in Chapter 4, language in SCT is perceived as an important symbolic tool. It is used to communicate information by the feedback provider to the writer (in feedback comments) and by the writer to process the feedback received. When processing feedback, learners use self-directed talk to draw attention to the feedback provided, to consider, question and explain the reasons for the feedback received. In doing so, they transform thinking into artifactual forms which in turn become available for further reflection (Swain, 2006a, 2006b). When deliberating about language (i.e. engaging in languaging) learners can create new knowledge and/or deepen their understanding of language conventions and language use.

In order to investigate how language is used as a mediational tool to process written CF, some researchers have used recorded pair talk as their data sources. In these studies (e.g. Brooks & Swain, 2009; Storch & Wigglesworth, 2010a, 2010b; Swain & Lapkin, 2002; Tocalli-Beller & Swain, 2005) the students typically receive feedback on their joint writing, and in responding to this feedback they may engage in two types of languaging: other-directed talk (i.e. talk directed to their peers) and self-directed talk (thinking out aloud in the presence of another person). These forms of languaging represent spontaneous verbalisation of the cognitive processes involved in processing feedback. Other researchers (e.g. Suzuki, 2012) have asked students to write down their reaction to the feedback received. This is a form of written think aloud protocols. Table 5.1 summarises the studies that investigated the nature and impact of languaging (using language as a tool to process the written CF) on revised drafts. The table presents information about the research design, the type of data collected and how it was analysed, and the main findings.

Table 5.1 Studies investigating the nature and impact of languaging

Studies	Participants	Research design	Data & Analysis	Findings
Swain & Lapkin (2002)	1 pair Grade 7 French immersion	4-stage study: 1. Joint writing 2. Noticing reformulation 3. Stimulated recall 4. Revision	Learners' engagement with written CF (Session 2) Revised version	Most reformulations noticed 67% of reformulations incorporated in revised version
Tocalli-Beller & Swain (2005)	12 Grade 7 French immersion	4-stage study as in Swain & Lapkin (2002)	Session 3 (stimulated recall recordings): Occasions of cognitive conflict Revised version	Engaging with reformulations (cognitive conflict) > just accepting reformulations
Adams (2003)	56 learners of Spanish	3 groups: 1. Noticing = compare own to reformulated version then repeat task 2. Noticing + stimulated recall then repeat task 3. Control group (task repetition, no feedback)	Accuracy of repeated tasks No. of reformulations incorporated correctly in repeated task	Gp 1 & 2 > control group on repeated task Gp 2 > Gp 1 incorporation of target like forms in repeated task

(Continued)

Studies	Participants	Research design	Data & Analysis	Findings
Storch & Wigglesworth (2007, 2010a, 2010b); Wigglesworth & Storch 2012); Storch (2010)	48 ESL Australia advanced	3 sessions, 2 groups: 1. Joint writing 2. Feedback + noticing + joint revision (= immediate post-test) Gp 1: reform Gp 2: editing 3. Individual revision (= delayed post- test)	Nature of pair talk (LREs) original texts vs. revised texts in Sessions 2 & 3 Case studies: analysis of pair discourse	Editing > reformulations: quantity & quality of LREs, uptake of feedback (Storch & Wigglesworth, 2010a) Retention of Reformulated feedback > editing (Storch, 2010) Retention of reformulations due to memorisation (Storch & Wigglesworth, 2010a, 2010b)
Suzuki (2012)	24 Japanese EFL, intermediate	3 stages: 1. Essay writing 2. Written reflections in L1 on feedback received= written languaging 3. Revision of original essay	Compare initial and revised essay Nature of written languaging Effect of written languaging on revisions	Structures on which learners reflected (Written languaging) incorporated in revised essay Higher accuracy on structures when learners understood why corrected

A series of studies conducted by a team of researchers led by Swain (Swain & Lapkin, 2002; Tocalli-Beller & Swain, 2005) had 12 grade 7 French immersion students involved in a multiple stage study over a two-week period. The research design was the same as that used in the study by Brooks and Swain (2009), discussed earlier, which involved learners in four distinct sessions. These studies are largely descriptive, providing abundant examples of episodes in which learners reflect consciously on language use and the impact this has, if at all, on the revised drafts.

The study by Swain and Lapkin (2002) focused on the talk of one case study pair. The researchers analysed the data in Sessions 2 and 3 for language related episodes (LREs – see Swain & Lapkin, 1995, 1998), noting the focus of these episodes, and whether the learners accepted or rejected the reformulations (see discussion in Section 5.3 on studies informed by activity theory). The study found that the learners noticed most of the reformulations, and seemed to pay more attention to grammar than to lexis or discourse. Analysis of the revised versions revealed that a large proportion (67%) of the amendments made by the learners corresponded to the reformulations. Thus the researchers concluded that reformulation was an effective feedback technique because the learners had multiple opportunities (in Sessions 2 and 3) to reflect on and engage with the feedback provided – that is, to language.

Tocalli-Beller and Swain (2005) used the data set from the Swain and Lapkin (2002) study and analysed occasions of cognitive conflict found in Session 3 of the study (the stimulated recall). Cognitive conflict is defined as an intellectual conflict that may facilitate learning because it leads to a discussion of different points of view. In the data, such conflict was evident in episodes where the learners questioned and sometimes disagreed with the expert feedback provided in the reformulations. Using the revised versions produced in Session 4, the researchers traced the effect of the cognitive conflict on the revisions made. They found that when students questioned the reformulations, and discussed them with the researcher, in the majority of cases this resulted in improved revisions. In contrast, when the students simply accepted the reformulations rather than questioning it, the errors persisted. Thus, the findings suggest that languaging in the form of questioning and discussion with the researcher led to a greater understanding because the learners had to verbalise their thoughts and question their own knowledge. They engaged in explanations, questioning, stating agreements and disagreements, and in the process constructed new knowledge or strengthened existing knowledge about language. This other-directed talk (with the researcher) mediated their learning: it was appropriated and used by the learners as their own resources when revising independently (Session 4).

In the above studies, as noted, processing of written CF took place in two sessions: when the learners compared their version of a text to that reformulated by a native speaker, and then in a stimulated recall session in which they tried to explain the reasons for their acceptance or deliberations about the reformulations. Adams (2003) replicated the Swain and Lapkin (2002) study, but used a modified research design. She compared the impact of noticing of the feedback provided via reformulation (the noticing group) with that of the stimulated recall (the noticing + stimulated recall group) by investigating the impact of the types of treatment on a repeated task. Adams also had a control group that simply repeated the task but received no feedback. The study found that although both treatment groups performed better on the repeated task compared to a control group, the noticing plus stimulated recall group significantly outperformed the noticing only group. The noticing plus stimulated recall group incorporated more of the feedback (reformulations) in the repeated task. Although treating repeated tasks as post-tests is questionable, these results show that the greater opportunities to language afforded by the recall session positively affected the learners' uptake of the written CF.

A large-scale research project conducted by Wigglesworth and Storch (see Storch & Wigglesworth, 2010a, 2010b; Wigglesworth & Storch, 2012) and informed by the research conducted by Swain and Lapkin (2002), also focused on the processing and uptake of feedback provided to advanced ESL learners on their joint writing. However, unlike the research design in Swain and Lapkin (2002), this project did not have a stimulated recall session. The participants attended three sessions. In Session 1 they produced a joint text. In Session 2 (five days later), they were given feedback on their joint text, discussed the feedback and then revised their text together (feedback removed). This session was treated as an immediate post-test. In Session 3, 28 days later, the participants revised the originally co-authored text, but did so individually. This final session was treated as a delayed post-test. One group received written CF in the form of editing symbols; the other in the form of reformulations. All pair talk was audio recorded, and transcripts were analysed for LREs, including the focus of the LREs, and the level of learners' engagement in resolving the LREs.

In one of the published papers from a subset of the data, Storch and Wigglesworth (2010a) reported on the data of 24 pairs. The study compared the number and nature of the LREs in response to the type of written CF (reformulations vs. editing symbols) and then examined whether it affected the immediately revised texts (produced in Session 2). The study found that written CF in the form of editing elicited a greater quantity and lengthier LREs than reformulations; that it encouraged learners to search and evaluate different alternatives; and that they often deliberated on language items beyond those on which they received feedback. The study also found that students who received editing feedback incorporated more of the feedback in their jointly revised texts than students who received reformulations. The researchers attributed their results to the deeper processing of written CF that editing symbols encouraged as evident in the pair talk. For advanced learners, these results suggest that editing or more implicit forms of written CF may elicit more languaging and culminate in more incorporation of the feedback provided in revised texts. Intuitively, this would suggest that more implicit forms of written CF might be more facilitative of L2 learning.

However, a comparison of the original texts (produced in Session 1), the revised texts completed after the processing of the feedback (Session 2) and the individually revised texts produced in Session 3 (see Storch, 2010a) showed that in fact gains (retention of the feedback) were more enduring for students who received reformulations. A closer analysis of the data using a case study approach (Storch & Wigglesworth, 2010a, 2010b) revealed a possible reason for the findings: learners memorised the reformulated text and were able to reproduce it even after 28 days. The analysis thus suggested the need to examine more closely learners' actions and what drives their actions when we consider the impact of written CF on students' writing (see discussion in Section 5.3 on activity theory).

As mentioned previously, learners' engagement or languaging with written CF has, by and large, been examined when the learners deliberate orally on the feedback they receive. Two studies have explored written forms of languaging in response to written CF. The first study, by Suzuki and Itagaki (2007), elicited retrospective reflections on feedback given to Japanese EFL writers on grammar exercises (translation and scrambled sentences). The second study by Suzuki (2012) elicited concurrent deliberations on feedback received. Given concerns about the correspondence between cognitive processes and retrospections (Gass & Mackey, 2000; Swain, 2006b), it is only Suzuki's (2012) study that will be considered here.

Suzuki's (2012) classroom study involved 24 Japanese learners of EFL of intermediate proficiency. The study had three stages. In Stage 1 the learners wrote essays on which they received direct feedback a week later (Stage 2). In this second stage the learners also produced written reflections (languaging) on the feedback they received. The corrected essays were then removed, and Stage 3 involved the learners in revising their original essays. In the written languaging phase of the study (Stage 2), the participants were asked to write explanations for why they thought their language forms (grammatical structures and lexical choices) were corrected. The participants also had the option to write 'don't know'. All written languaging was done in the students' L1. The researcher then compared the initial and revised essays for the effect of written languaging.

The study found that when participants understood why their language was corrected (evident in the languaging episodes) they were more likely to incorporate the corrections in their revised drafts than if they were unsure why they were corrected ('don't know' episodes). This is an interesting finding given that a number of researchers have reported a tendency by students to incorporate teacher feedback in their revisions, even if they do not understand it (see for example the discussion of Zhao's 2010 study in Section 5.1.2). Suzuki suggests that providing learners with opportunities to reflect about their linguistic knowledge facilitated the learners' L2 development. However, as the author admits, given that the learners produced revised rather than new essays, the fairly short interval between the languaging task and the revision task, and that there was no control group, the claims concerning the impact of written languaging on language learning are tentative and require more robust empirical evidence.

Taken together, the studies suggest that learners' deliberations about the written CF they receive, whether in oral form (via discussions with peers or with the feedback provider) or written form (written languaging), may lead to improved performance on revised drafts. These deliberations are a form of languaging – using language to notice and acknowledge the feedback, to understand or to question why the feedback was given. The studies discussed suggest that languaging may enhance the retention of the written CF and thus improve the accuracy of revised texts. However, what most of these studies lack is evidence showing that learners can use the knowledge they co-constructed (with tutors or peers) as a resource in independent performance on new writing. This is the area that future studies need to pursue; that is, we need to investigate the role of language as a tool that mediates language learning following written CF.

5.2.2   The impact of material tools: Computer-mediated written CF

Another area of investigation related to mediation and tools is how new tools, namely computer-mediated means of providing and delivering feedback, shape the feedback comments, the processing of the feedback, and the impact on revision and language learning. Much of this research has focused on feedback provided by peers in peer response activities, comparing traditional and electronic ways of providing peer feedback (e.g. Liu & Sadler, 2003; Schultz, 2000), or the effect of different communication technologies on peer interaction and subsequent revisions (e.g. AbuSeileek, 2013; Jin & Zhu, 2010; Liang, 2010). It should also be noted that most of these studies tend to make only a cursory reference to theories of language learning (including SCT, e.g. AbuSeileek & Abualsha'r, 2014; Liang, 2010; Yeh & Lo, 2009). Therefore, although some of these studies are discussed in this section, they are not studies which were informed by SCT in their design, and nor do their authors refer to SCT (or indeed any other theory) when discussing and explaining their findings.

Studies investigating teacher-written CF delivered electronically are few in number and not well designed. For example, Tafazoli *et al.* (2014)

compared written CF delivered to learners via email and in paper form. In this relatively large-scale study (N=86), two groups of EFL learners in Iran received explicit written CF (correct forms inserted) on seven successive assignments. One group wrote their essays using Microsoft Word and received their feedback via email exchanges, the other wrote their essays using pen and paper and received feedback on their hard copies in class. A post-test (writing completed by all participants at the end of the study) showed a statistically significant reduction in the number of errors in the writing of students who received emailed feedback compared to those who received conventionally delivered feedback. However, it is not clear why email delivery of feedback proved superior to pen and paper. There was no indication of how the learners engaged with the feedback received in the two modes or indeed the quantity and quality of the feedback given. A confounding factor, which was not considered by the researchers, was the mode of composing, given that one group composed on paper and the other on the computer. The authors admit that their findings could be due to the impact of the novelty of using computers on learners' motivation to write (and thereby probably to revise).

Yeh and Lo (2009) designed an online corrective feedback system, entitled Online Annotator, which allows teachers to mark up learners' writing by drawing on a bank of error codes. The system can also display a summary of error types made by the writer in any one document or in successive documents. In order to examine the efficacy of the system, the researchers compared the performance of two groups of EFL writers in Taiwan. Unlike Tafazoli *et al*.'s (2014) study, in this study all participants submitted their essays online. One group (experimental group) received corrective feedback using the Online Annotator system, the other on printed copies of their writing. The students also completed an editing task and a new piece of writing at the end of the study. However, only performance on the editing task was analysed. The researchers found that the experimental group performed better on the editing task in terms of identifying errors. Since there was no pre-test and no analysis of the new writing task, as well as no information about the quantity and nature of the feedback given in the two modes, it is hard to attribute the better test performance of the experimental group to the use of the Online Annotator as a tool to deliver written CF.

There is a much larger body of research on the impact of peer feedback delivered electronically. Overall, these studies seem to be better designed than the studies on computer-mediated written CF provided by teachers, yet they are still largely descriptive. Table 5.2 summarises these studies, providing details of the tools used to deliver the computer-mediated written CF and the findings in terms of amount of feedback provided, engagement with the feedback, and impact on revisions.

Table 5.2 Studies investigating computer-mediated peer written CF

Studies	Participants	Material tools	Findings
Liu & Sadler (2003)	8 Advanced ESL	1. Hard copies + face-to-face conference 2. Track changes + Chat	Amount of feedback: GP 2>Gp1 Engagement: more direct feedback in Gp 1; Interactions in Gp 2 superficial Revisions: Gp 2>Gp 1
Schulz (2000)	3 groups, French FL	1. Face to face 2. MSN Messenger 3. Mixed mode	Engagement: superficial, esp. lower proficiency learners Revisions: depends on proficiency
Guardado & Shi (2007)	22 ESL, Canada	Discussion board chat to deliver feedback	Engagement: reluctant to engage Few revisions
Liang (2010)	12 EFL, Taiwan	Groups of 4 (mixed proficiency), longitudinal, combine face-to-face and online chat	Chat: rare error correction, most talk social Revisions: mixed depending on group dynamics
Chang (2012)	24 EFL, Taiwan	1. Face to face 2. MSN Messenger (synchronous) 3. Discussion Board (asynchronous)	Engagement: less intensive in computer-mediated mode
AbuSeileek & Abualsha'r (2014)	64 Intermediate EFL, Saudi Arabia	1. Track changes 2. Comment function to provide direct corrections 3. Comment function to provide metalinguisitic feedback 4. Control (no feedback) Pre- & post-test	Gp 1 > 2, 3 & 4 on post-test

An early study by Liu and Sadler (2003) compared two modes of providing peer feedback. The small-scale study of advanced ESL learners had one group (n=4) exchanging peer comments on hard copies followed by a face-to-face conference; the other group (n=4) exchanging comments using the track changes in Microsoft Word followed by chat interactions in Moos (Multi-user domains object-orientated). The study found that the computer-enhanced group provided almost twice the number of feedback comments than the traditional group. Furthermore, the computer-enhanced group tended to provide explicit or direct written CF, whereas the traditional group provided more indirect feedback (clarification requests). The authors attributed the nature of the feedback to the tool: to the ease of providing feedback, particularly direct written CF, in the computer-enhanced form.

Investigations of different modes of delivering peer feedback yielded some interesting findings in terms of students' interactions. Liu and Sadler (2003) reported that in comparison to traditional face-to-face interactions, the interactions (chats) in Moos were often superficial, disjointed and off-task, with the potential to be easily misinterpreted. Schultz (2000) also observed a tendency to veer off-task in online synchronous chats (using MSN Messenger[1]), and for the interaction to be quite formulaic, particularly among lower proficiency learners, in comparison to more recursive interactions found in the transcripts of recorded face-to-face peer interactions. Guardado and Shi (2007), who used Discussion Board, an asynchronous chat function of Blackboard (a course management application) to deliver peer feedback, reported that learners were reluctant to engage with the feedback comments posted. Among the reasons given by the participants in follow-up interviews for this reluctance was the extra effort required in online communication compared to the immediacy of face-to-face interactions and the anonymity of the comments. The participants commented that although the anonymity enabled them to be more critical in their feedback than in face-to-face peer response activities, it discouraged interaction. The students felt uncomfortable seeking clarifications on comments provided by an anonymous peer. This made the peer response activity a one-way communication process.

One of the criticisms that can be levelled at these peer feedback studies is the contrived nature of the context used for online communication. Many of the studies (e.g. Guardado & Shi, 2007; Liang, 2010; Liu & Sadler, 2003) had learners working in close physical proximity when providing computer-mediated peer feedback; that is, they were in the same computer laboratory when they chatted online or sent messages to each other. One could argue that this close proximity obviated the need to interact. However, Chang's (2012) study, which had the computer-mediated forms of feedback occurring outside class time, also found limited interaction among peers in the computer-mediated mode of communication, particularly in the asynchronous Discussion Board, compared to the face-to-face mode.

Findings about the impact of the tools used to provide feedback on revisions are mixed. Some studies report that the computer-mediated feedback encouraged more revisions (e.g. the track changes used in Liu & Sadler, 2003); others report fewer revisions because of lack of engagement with the feedback (e.g. Guardado & Shi, 2007) or mixed findings depending on the proficiency of the learners (e.g. Schultz, 2000), and the group dynamics (e.g. Liang, 2010). Few studies report on the impact of different means of providing peer feedback on language learning (i.e. new texts), with the exception of AbuSeileek and Abualsha'r (2014).

The longitudinal study by AbuSeileek and Abualsha'r (2014) set out to compare the efficacy of three forms of providing computer-enhanced peer corrective feedback: track changes, using the comment function of Microsoft Word to provide direct corrective feedback, and using this comment function to provide metalinguistic feedback (e.g. subject-verb agreement). It should be noted that all three treatment groups had face-to-face sessions to discuss the feedback. The study, using a pre-post-test design, found that the group that received track changes outperformed the two other groups (as well as a control group) even though the amount of feedback and focus of the feedback (on grammatical accuracy) was similar in all three treatment conditions. The authors attributed the findings to the visual saliency of track changes in identifying errors and enabling learners to make cognitive comparisons between the reformulated and erroneous versions. There is no mention of what impact the three forms of providing feedback had on the ensuing face-to-face interactions.

Overall, there is clearly a need for more and better designed studies which investigate the impact of feedback provided by teachers in computer-mediated modes. Such studies need to compare the frequency and nature of the feedback in different modes of delivery, learners' engagement with that feedback, and ultimately its impact on writing development. Studies on teacher feedback need to heed what we can learn from studies on computer-mediated peer feedback.

Findings of peer feedback studies suggest that the physical tool used to provide feedback affects feedback practices. Computer-mediated tools may increase the amount and nature of the feedback, and more importantly perhaps, the way learners interact discursively with each other, which may differ to how they interact with each other in face-to-face encounters. The research suggests that these forms of virtual communication may discourage interaction, or substantive interaction, and thus may not be conducive to language learning. Indeed most of the authors of these studies on peer feedback (e.g. Guardado & Shi, 2007; Liu & Sadler, 2003; Schultz, 2000) conclude by recommending that teachers combine computer-mediated feedback with face-to-face peer interactions, rather than treating them as alternatives, in order to provide peer feedback in a more personalised and interactive environment. Chang (2012) argues that the different modes of providing peer feedback may accommodate individual preferences. Her interview data shows that individual student preferences may guide their feedback behaviour, regardless of the mode used. Research findings presented in the next section reinforce the need to consider students as individuals when attempting to explain their behaviour.

5.3   Activity Theory: Feedback as an Activity

Research informed by AT attempts to explain the behaviour of feedback providers and of feedback receivers (the subjects in the activity). The theoretical framework provides a way to interpret human behaviour by trying to view it as an activity driven and defined by motives and realised by goal directed actions. Actions are further shaped by context-specific dimensions, including personal, institutional and interpersonal dimensions. As a number of scholars have pointed out, context-specific dimensions have been largely ignored in research on written CF (Goldstein, 2001; Hyland & Hyland, 2006a, 2006b; Lee 2014).

The studies discussed in this section are divided into three subsections. The first subsection discusses studies that have investigated the actions of feedback receivers (learners) who may accept, ignore or reject the feedback offered by the experts (teachers). The second subsection looks at studies that have investigated the actions of the experts – the feedback providers – focusing on why they implement particular feedback practices in their specific teaching environment. The third subsection discusses studies on peer feedback in peer response tasks.

Although a review of the literature shows evidence that sociocultural theory has informed a growing number of studies on written CF in the past two decades, this is not the case with AT. To date, only three studies on written CF have been informed by AT, all investigating peer feedback (see Section 5.3.3). Thus, as in the previous section (5.2.2), in selecting studies to discuss in the following subsections, we have included studies that make reference to SCT but not AT (e.g. Macqueen, 2012; Swain & Lapkin, 2002; Zhao, 2010) as well as studies which, although they make no reference to SCT or AT, they nevertheless situate their investigations in real classrooms, provide rich contextual data, and discuss their findings with reference to their context (e.g. F. Hyland, 1998, 2011; Lee, 2008a, 2009; Min, 2013). At the same time, we excluded a small number of studies (e.g. Mustafa, 2012) that despite making a reference to SCT, the research design and discussion did not demonstrate the main tenets of the theory.

5.3.1   Learners' response to teachers' written CF

In this section we review studies that have attempted to explain learners' response to feedback viewed as a form of social action taken by learners as volitional agents. These actions are driven by their personal goals and beliefs about L2 writing that are grounded in their previous educational experiences. The aim of these studies is to explain the outcomes of the activity; that is, why only some of the feedback may be noticed, incorporated into revised drafts and internalised by learners to be ultimately used as their own linguistic resources (in new writing). As in research on language as a mediational tool, discussed in Section 5.2.2, the studies discussed in this section use qualitative data elicited, for example, from pair talk, interviews and detailed observations.

The studies by Swain and Lapkin (2002) and Storch and Wigglesworth (2010a, 2010b), discussed in previous sections, investigated primarily how learners processed the written CF they received on their joint writing. However, what became evident in the learners' talk is that learners may choose to reject the feedback given by an expert (a native speaker). For example, Swain and Lapkin (2002), using the talk of one case study pair, provided evidence of learners explicitly rejecting some of the feedback or questioning its veracity because it did not accord with a rule they had already internalised, or where they felt that the alternative provided changed their intended meaning.

Similar findings were reported by Macqueen (2012) in a longitudinal study with four ESL informants. The informants were interviewed retrospectively after each feedback cycle whereby the students wrote, received feedback and revised their text. Macqueen used these retrospective interviews with each participant and a lexical trail analysis that involved tracing the use of certain words and strings of words in the students' writing over time. The study found that some patterns of language use were resistant to change despite the feedback provided because of the strength of earlier priming.

Storch and Wigglesworth (2010a, 2010b, see also Wigglesworth & Storch, 2012) showed that although feedback provided by the expert may be noticed, learners exercising their agency might choose not to incorporate it in their revised drafts. Storch and Wigglesworth (2010a, 2010b) also found instances where feedback was questioned, and thus although it was incorporated in the immediate revised draft, it was not internalised. Therefore, it was not used in the post-test (individual revision). The authors suggest that feedback that is noticed but not understood may lead to revisions but not necessarily to writing development (see also Tocalli-Beller & Swain, 2005).

The above studies provide a snapshot of the feedback activity – focusing mainly on learners' processing of feedback received on one occasion from a researcher. The studies by Zhao (2010), Lee (2008a) and F. Hyland (1998) were longitudinal and investigated students' reactions to the feedback they received in authentic language classes. Using different sources of data (interviews, observations, samples of writing) they showed how contextual factors influenced students' response to the feedback.

Zhao's (2010) study, discussed earlier, conducted with EFL learners in China, investigated, among other issues, learners' response to teacher (and peer) feedback. Of particular interest here was the finding that a relatively large proportion (42%) of incorporated teacher feedback comments were not understood by the students. Interview data and classroom observations suggested that in this context students were reluctant to question or challenge the teacher's authority or expertise. Zhu argues that researchers need to examine not only whether learners incorporate teacher feedback but also why and whether they understand it.

Lee's (2008a) study was conducted in two Hong Kong secondary classrooms, an educational context similar to that described by Zhao (2010). The study examined the reaction of two classes of students, one class of high proficiency English learners, the other of low proficiency learners. The students' writing showed that the teachers provided comprehensive feedback (in line with the schools' policies), predominantly on language errors, and that the feedback was mainly in the form of overt corrections. The students' responses, elicited via questionnaires and feedback protocols, showed that the lower proficiency students seemed less interested in the written CF than the higher proficiency students, and that they did not always understand the feedback. Lee links this response not only to the learners' L2 proficiency but also to the nature of the teachers' approach in the classes immediately after the feedback was provided. The teacher teaching the more proficient students was observed to be more encouraging; the teacher teaching the less proficient students seemed to adopt a discouraging and oppressive approach. Thus the study shows that how feedback is delivered and the pedagogical context in which it is delivered influence students' response to the feedback. Despite the fact that the study was longitudinal (data collected over an entire academic year), there was no analysis of the students' successive writing assignments (students only wrote one draft and were not required to revise) to examine whether the feedback provided had an impact, if any, on L2 development.

F. Hyland's longitudinal study (1998), conducted with ESL learners in New Zealand, shows not only how and why learners respond to written CF in successive drafts but also the potential long-term impact that written CF can have on the learners' self-perceptions and confidence as L2 writers. In a number of subsequent publications (e.g. 2003, 2011) F. Hyland reported on the focus of the feedback given by the teachers, showing that it mostly focused on form (2003), and the views of six case study ESL learners regarding written CF (2011). However, of most relevance here is the detailed account on two of the learners reported in the 1998 publication, and on another learner in the 2011 publication.

In the 1998 publication, the two case study learners, Maho and Samorn, began the semester with positive attitudes to L2 writing and teacher-written feedback. By the end of the semester, their attitudes changed because of their experience with feedback on their writing and how it aligned with their goals, beliefs and expectations. Maho, the weaker student, viewed writing as a means to communicate her ideas. Her overriding desire was to express her intended meaning and thus she preferred feedback on her ideas rather than on the accuracy of her expression. She also strongly believed that the act of writing helped her to develop her ideas. Thus, instead of revising, she rewrote large chunks of her text largely ignoring the corrective feedback and advice she received from her teacher. At the end of the writing course she felt that her writing did not improve. Samorn, the more proficient student, viewed grammatical accuracy as very important in good writing and wanted the teacher to provide feedback on all her errors, and the teacher indeed obliged. In revising her writing, she followed very closely the feedback she received. Yet the teacher's focus on areas that needed improvement and the lack of any positive feedback on Samorn's language use, the kind of feedback that Samorn was accustomed to receive in her home country, over time led Samorn to lose confidence in her writing ability and her mastery of grammar.

The other learner, Keith, reported on in the 2011 publication, presents a more positive case. Keith's language proficiency was intermediate, and he was mainly concerned with his grammatical inaccuracies. Keith began the course with very clear ideas about the role of the teacher and the feedback. He believed that the teacher should provide feedback on all his errors, but preferred indirect feedback (using underlining and symbols) that encouraged students to play a more active role in their corrections. Keith was a very proactive learner: he regularly consulted other sources of information (peers, dictionaries and grammar books, self-access centre); he kept a log of his errors, and experimented with complex vocabulary and grammatical structures in his drafts in order to get feedback on his attempts. This sustained active engagement in the language learning process seemed to have paid off. His writing showed gradual improvement and he felt very proud about his progress.

These case studies show that learners are not passive recipients of written CF. The case study learners were well aware of their own L2 writing goals, held strong beliefs shaped by their previous learning experiences about the kind of feedback that best addressed their needs, and responded to the feedback according to these goals and beliefs. The studies also show that a mismatch between what learners expect and what they receive in terms of written CF may have an adverse effect on their confidence and ability to write in the L2. Such important insights can be revealed only in longitudinal case studies that go beyond questionnaire data and an examination of the written product.

5.3.2   Teachers' written CF practices

A number of studies have investigated teachers' feedback practices, looking at the kind of feedback teachers give and why. These studies have reported that teachers adopt a range of approaches to the provision of written corrective feedback (see Evans *et al.*, 2010) and that their approaches are influenced by a host of factors, including their beliefs about the efficacy of certain types of feedback. These studies, however, have also yielded mixed findings about whether teachers' espoused beliefs and self-reported perceptions converge with their actual practices. While some studies report a close convergence (e.g. Ferris, 2014), many others show a lack of convergence particularly in terms of the quantity and type of feedback provided (e.g. Al Shahrani & Storch, 2014; Hyland, 2011; Lee, 2009; Montgomery & Baker, 2007). Research has also shown that the type of written CF teachers give may not accord with what their students prefer (e.g. Amrhein & Nassaji, 2008; McMartin-Miller, 2014), and that teachers may not always be aware of their students' preferences (Al Shahrani & Storch, 2014).

However, these studies tend to draw on surveys (e.g. Evans *et al.*, 2010) and interviews conducted at one point of time (e.g. Ferris, 2014), and although they may be supplemented by an analysis of teachers' feedback on students' texts, they nevertheless provide a very general and static description of teachers' feedback practices. Research informed by SCT or activity theory expands the scope of this research by looking at what individual teachers actually do in a specific teaching context and why, and whether teachers' feedback practices change over time and why. From an AT perspective, teacher feedback practices are, as in the case of learners' response to feedback, driven by their goals and beliefs. Teachers' feedback practices may also be influenced by the sociocultural and personal dimensions of the context, such as, for example, the relationships teachers form with their students or the expectations imposed by key stakeholders. The studies discussed in this subsection are longitudinal case studies that employed a range of research tools in order to capture the reality of the context in which the feedback takes place.

Lee's (2008b) study analysed the feedback provided by 26 Hong Kong secondary school teachers and followed this analysis with interviews of a subset of the teachers (six teachers). What distinguished this study from other studies employing interviews and text analysis (e.g. Ferris, 2014) is that it was conducted in a specific educational context and identified factors specific to that context that influenced the teachers' behaviour. The study found that the feedback the teachers provided was predominantly CF and direct (providing the correct answers). This pattern seemed to contravene the recommendations of the Hong Kong educational authorities. The interview data revealed the reasons for this disjuncture. The study found that the teachers' practices were influenced to some extent by their beliefs but more so by context-related factors, particularly the power exerted by the local school authorities. The schools expected teachers to provide feedback on errors rather than other aspects of writing, and to provide comprehensive corrective feedback. The schools closely checked the teachers' practices to ensure that they complied with their policies, with compliance reports used in the teachers' performance appraisals. Lack of compliance had detrimental employment consequences. A strong exam culture with a heavy focus on accuracy in exam grading reinforced teachers' feedback behaviour. All key stakeholders (administrators, students and their parents) expected teachers to provide comprehensive written CF in the belief that this kind of feedback would improve the students' performance on the exams.

In 2014, Lee used AT to describe and interpret her earlier findings. The feedback activity can be said to have taken place within **a community** whose members comprise the teachers, school administrators, students and their parents. The school policies concerning appropriate written CF are the **rules** within the activity system; and the power exercised by authorities in the appraisal system demonstrates the **division of labour.** These rules and power relations make it difficult for teachers to use alternative approaches to the provision of CF, even if they believe that the expected and enforced approaches are ineffective. The hierarchical power structures in the schools disempower teachers in this community. Thus using the lens of AT, Lee shows that teachers' feedback practices, like all human activities, are embedded and shaped by the cultural and institutional dimensions of a particular context. Lee also uses the G_2 framework of AT (reproduced below as Figure 5.2) to identify the required changes. These changes include transforming the **object** that drives teachers' feedback practices and students' response, the **actions** (e.g. targeted feedback, multiple drafts, revisions), the **rules** and **the division of labour** (e.g. who determines feedback policies, how policies are enacted). Lee argues that in this transformed system, teachers and students can become active agents in the activity with greater autonomy.

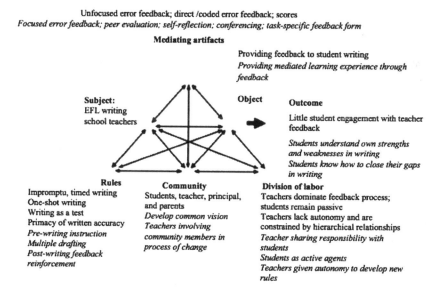

Figure 5.2 Using AT to map a feedback activity system in an EFL writing class in Hong Kong and possible innovations (reproduced with permission from Lee, 2014)

Studies conducted in contexts where teachers have more autonomy in the kind of feedback they provide their learners, have investigated how teachers' actions are affected by their beliefs as well as how their students respond to their feedback. These longitudinal studies have also investigated changes, if any, in the teachers' feedback behaviour over time, and thus provide a more dynamic perspective of the written CF activity.

Min's (2013) study is a critical reflective self-inquiry of the teacher's/researcher's own beliefs and practices concerning feedback on writing, including corrective feedback. The data was collected over a semester in Taiwan, in an EFL writing class taught by Min. Unlike the Morton *et al.* (2014) and Storch (2014) studies discussed earlier, this study included not only successive students' written assignments with teacher commentary but also the teacher's entries in a reflection journal and learning logs. Because the original purpose of the journal and logs was to document the implementation of peer feedback activities, Min argues that these entries provide uncontaminated data. Min found that her beliefs changed over the semester, with a shift from attempting to identify and respond to all problems in the students' writing to a desire to understand their intention. This shift was also reflected in her feedback comments, which increasingly took a more probing stance rather than the prescriptive stance adopted initially. These changes in her goals and actions were attributed to the insights gained from professional reading, conferences and observations of her students' reactions to the feedback they received.

Hyland and Hyland (2006a), drawing on the data collected by F. Hyland (1998), provide some glimpses of teacher decision-making processes when giving corrective feedback. Using think aloud protocol data, they show that teachers' decisions about the kind of feedback to give and what to focus on in their feedback were influenced by the teachers' own pedagogical goals and perceived roles (e.g. gatekeepers, experts on language use) and also by their conceptualisation of the student. The teachers responded not merely to the errors but also to the learner who made the errors, taking into consideration the learner's evolving writing needs and response to feedback provided on previous writing. The study thus shows that feedback is a reciprocal activity, where the actions of one group of subjects in the activity influence and are influenced by the actions of another group. The reciprocity of this activity is most clearly illustrated in the study by Lee and Schallert (2008).

Lee and Schallert (2008) analysed the dynamic interaction of all aspects of the activity of giving and responding to feedback. As such the study provides a clear example of the third generation of AT, proposed by Engeström (2001) (see Chapter 4). Although the authors refer to sociocultural rather than activity theory in their article, we discuss the study by reference to activity theory, encoding their findings with terms used in AT in order to exemplify how the theory can be employed in research on written CF using the more complex model of AT.

Lee and Schallert's (2008) longitudinal case study was conducted in an intensive six-week summer English writing course in a Korean university. Data was collected via classroom observations, formal and informal interviews, recordings of teacher-student conferences and five students' assignments, including first drafts with teacher feedback commentary (on all aspects of their writing) and revised drafts. This multitude of sources, as in the case of F. Hyland's study (1998), yielded rich data. The case study informants (the **subjects** in the activity) included the female teacher (Dr Kim) and two male students (Sangho and Jongmin), who were selected from a larger pool as they provided interesting and contrasting cases. Dr Kim was a non-native but highly proficient speaker of English who completed her PhD in English literature in a Korean university. She provided extensive feedback on her students' writing, on both first and final drafts, believing that the feedback and the redrafting would improve her students' academic English writing, her ultimate goal.

The two male students had different language learning histories and different reasons for enrolling in the writing class. These individual histories and goals shaped the relationship the two case study participants formed with the teacher, and how they responded to the feedback she provided. Sangho had learnt English in Korea, and identified himself as a poor writer. He enrolled in the English course to improve his English writing (**object**) in order to pursue further studies abroad. He recognised the English teacher as an expert in teaching English writing, and thus trusted and valued her detailed and precise feedback on all his writing. Being a diligent student, he paid close attention to the feedback when revising his drafts (**actions**). His actions may have also been affected by the broader **community** and its specific cultural norms. Korean students are expected to be obedient (**division of labour**). Compliance is considered a mark of a good student. In return, the teacher appreciated his effort and praised his progress and writing abilities in her feedback (**teacher reciprocal action**).

The other student, Jongmin, had lived and attended school for a number of years in English-speaking countries. He considered himself a proficient and good writer in both English and Korean, but more so in English. He enrolled in the course for reasons of expediency. His main **object** was to gain credit by completing a short course during a summer semester. From the outset, he did not view the teacher as an expert in English because she had not studied outside Korea. Such views are apparently widespread in Korea and are reflected in discriminatory employment policies (**division of**

labour). His high estimation of his own English writing ability, his motive for enrolling and beliefs explain his response to the teacher's feedback (**actions**). He distrusted and challenged her feedback – a more accepted norm of behaviour (**rules**) in the Westernised countries in which he received his prior education. He put very little effort in his writing and revisions, often ignoring the teacher's feedback. The teacher continued to provide substantial feedback, partly due to obligation (**institutional rules**) but also to assert her expertise in teaching English writing. The feedback given was often negative and the grades low (**actions**), and this in turn further eroded Jongmin's trust in his teacher's English expertise.

Thus the study provides evidence of the complex and dynamic nature of the intersecting activity systems that take place within a broader social and cultural context. The human participants come into the activity with their own beliefs, expectations and objects, and these explain their actions. More importantly, it shows the co-constructed nature of the feedback activity: the participants' (teachers and students) feedback behaviour shapes and is shaped by each other.

5.3.3   The provision and response to peer feedback from an activity theory perspective

To date only three studies have analysed peer feedback using AT as their theoretical framework: Thorne (2004), Jin and Zhu (2010) and Zhu and Mitchell (2012). Whereas Jin and Zhu (2010) as well as Zhu and Mitchell (2012) focused mainly on learners' object/motive situated in the top tier of Leontiev's (1981) second generation (G_2) AT, Thorne (2004) analysed a peer response project as an entire activity system, using Engeström's (1987, 2001) G_2 version of AT.

Jin and Zhu's (2010) study investigated peer response behaviour in a computer-mediated environment. What distinguished this study from those discussed in Section 3.1, and which investigated the impact of material tools on learners' behaviour, is that this study examined the impact of tools on learners' motives, including the formation of new motives, in order to explain learners' behaviour. The study was longitudinal and conducted with advanced EAP students in an English language institute in the US. An impressive array of data sources was used: surveys, on- and off-screen behaviour captured by video cameras, recorded interviews conducted after each of the three peer response tasks, and the students' drafts and redrafts. The researchers triangulated all their data sources to present the contrasting experiences of two case study learners: Anton, a Belgian woman who was a confident user of instant messenger and Iron, a Turkish man who had no experience of using this tool. The two learners were partnered in the first two peer response tasks, but paired with new partners in the third task. Anton's behaviour on- and off-screen and interview responses indicated that she was very focused on giving and responding to her peer's feedback in the first peer response task, because she was driven by the motive to improve her writing. However, because she found Iron's lack of experience with messenger frustrating, during the second task she disengaged from the activity, providing Iron very little feedback and rejecting the feedback he provided. Instead, she exchanged off-task messages with her friends. Her motive became that of having fun. In the third task, paired with another learner, she was driven by two motives: to improve her writing (evident in her help-seeking behaviour) and having fun (exchanging unrelated messages with friends), in a sense participating in two activities simultaneously. Iron's motives also shifted over time: from being very task-focused, driven by a desire to improve his writing, to being driven by a desire to improve his instant messaging skills in the second task. In the third task, when partnered with another learner who appreciated his help, he began to enjoy the activity (giving rather than receiving feedback) because it restored his self-image as a competent person. Thus the study showed that the tool affected how the learners interacted and how it affected their motives by triggering the formation of new motives and abolishing existing motives.

In a subsequent study, Zhu, together with Mitchell (2012), examined peer feedback in a face-to-face environment. Again, using a case study approach, the researchers examined the behaviour of two Spanish-speaking female students in an EAP class as they participated in peer response tasks, each working in a different triad. The authors described the stances the learners adopted to their peers and to providing and receiving feedback, but unlike earlier descriptive studies (e.g. Guerrero & Villamil, 1994, 2000), Zhu and Mitchell also attempted to explain their learners' stances by reference to motives. The interview data showed that the learners were driven by different motives. Whereas one participant (Ingrid) was primarily driven by a desire to improve the quality of the text (hers and that of her peers), the other participant (Rosa) was motivated to improve her own language learning processes (via feedback on her writing and by adopting a tutor role when providing feedback). These motives affected their stances as writers and as reviewers and thus, although on the surface they appeared to engage in the same activity, their divergent motives meant that they carried out qualitatively different activities.

Thorne (2004) used the framework of AT (G_2) to map a peer response project in order to address the identified shortcomings of the project. In the project, a group of advanced L2 Spanish learners from one class were randomly paired with lower proficiency learners from another class. The higher proficiency learners (n=16) provided feedback (via emails) on grammar and content on essays written by lower proficiency learners (n=16). Although a very high proportion of the feedback provided was incorporated in the revised drafts, and both groups of students expressed high levels of satisfaction with the project, two shortcomings were identified: an overemphasis by the reviewers on grammatical errors at the expense of content comments and some comprehension difficulties experienced by the reviewers. By mapping all elements of the activity onto the framework of AT, Thorne identified the elements that could be modified to further improve the activity and its outcomes. These elements included the **rules** (increased frequency of encounters) to allow for clarifications by both reviewers and writers and **mediating artefacts** (augmenting emails with face-to-face encounters). Thorne suggested that such modifications could then potentially lead to another outcome: greater solidarity between the two groups.

In conclusion, the studies discussed in this section demonstrate quite vividly how individual variables (learner and teacher), context-specific variables, and the interaction of all these variables can help explain learners' response to written CF. The studies present participants as intentional human agents whose response to written CF may not be predictable and may change over time depending, in part, on the relationship they construct with the feedback provider.

Some of the variables investigated in these studies (goals, educational context) have also been considered by studies adopting a cognitive approach to research on written CF (discussed in Chapters 2 and 3). What perhaps distinguishes the studies informed by AT is their attempt to explore and explain behaviour rather than to prove hypotheses and hence the observed differences in their research design (case studies, qualitative data). Although these studies are often longitudinal, they do not always consider the impact of written CF on L2 development, an aspect that needs to be considered in future research. Nevertheless, the thickness and richness of the data in these studies provides us with an insight into the complexity of written CF as an activity. More importantly, perhaps, these studies suggest that the impact of written CF may go beyond L2 writing development, extending to L2 writer identity.

5.4 Concluding Remarks

The studies discussed in this chapter focus on the *why* question in research on feedback: *why* some feedback may be effective (notion of scaffolded feedback), and *why* students incorporate the feedback provided by teachers or peers by looking at how they process the feedback provided in traditional form or via computer-mediated means (tools), and what personal and contextual dimensions drive and explain their actions (activity theory). Teachers' feedback practices and that of peers in peer response tasks can also be explained by considering these dimensions and the interaction of these dimensions.

We noted at the outset that there are relatively few studies that have been informed by SCT (and AT). We also identified, when discussing the studies, that most of these studies do not include new pieces of students' writing. This is the research design feature that future studies informed by SCT and AT need to employ. The studies tend to be small-scale case studies. One of the criticisms often levelled at small-scale studies is the lack of generalizability of their findings (e.g. Davis, 1995). However, as Lee (2008a) points out, it is equally questionable whether decontextualised findings from larger-scale studies can be generalised to other learners and learning contexts. Such large-scale studies, as Goldstein (2001, 2006) argued, are often 'non-contextual and non-social, focused largely on texts and conducted within a linear model of teacher respond and student revise' (Goldstein, 2001: 77), which portray language learning as uni-directional rather than as social and dynamic activities (Goldstein, 2004, 2006; Murphy, 2000). The case studies discussed in this chapter have tended to provide thick descriptions of behaviour and of the context in which the feedback activity takes place. They show that teachers' written corrective feedback practices and students' responses are complex and multifaceted activity systems, and this may explain why we see inconclusive and mixed results in research on written CF.

In the final chapter we summarise the insights research informed by cognitive and SCT perspectives have provided us as teachers and researchers and outline future research directions. A future research agenda needs to consider not only written CF provided by humans but increasingly totally automated feedback. The impact of this tool on the provision and processing of feedback is clearly an area that requires carefully designed studies.

Note

(1) MSN messenger was discontinued in 2013.

6 Conclusion

6.0 Introduction

Our initial impetus for writing this book was our observation that despite the growing number of studies on written CF, what seemed to be absent in many of these studies was a theoretical framework that informed their research design and explained their findings. Most of the studies seemed to be driven by pedagogical questions, often ignoring what we know about second language learning processes. For examples, studies driven by a desire to show evidence of language gains after the single provision of a particular form of written CF seem to ignore the fact that SLA takes time and may not always be linear. Thus our main aim in writing this book was to provide an overview of the theories of L2 learning within the cognitive and sociocultural perspectives and consider to what extent they explain a role for written CF in L2 learning processes, as well as the possible explanations for why written CF may or may not lead to successful L2 development.

Although the field of SLA has generated a number of theories which attempt to explain L2 learning processes, we have chosen to focus primarily on two leading theoretical paradigms: cognitive and sociocultural. The choice was partially related to our own history as researchers, and the theoretical frameworks that have guided our research. Our choice was also based on a review of the empirical literature on written CF, and the observation that cognitive and sociocultural theoretical perspectives are most often mentioned in this body of research, if at all.

We begin this chapter (Section 6.1) with a summary of what these two theoretical perspectives, cognitive (6.1.1) and sociocultural (6.1.2), tell us about the potential role of written CF for successful L2 development, as well as what promotes (or impedes) the processing of the feedback and ultimately its internalisation (learning new knowledge or consolidating existing knowledge). We draw in our discussion on findings from research that has been informed by these theoretical perspectives, and note some of the existing shortcomings in this research. In the subsequent section (6.2), we focus on future research directions. This section is also divided into two subsections, summarising the kind of research needed from a cognitive perspective (6.2.1) and a sociocultural perspective (6.2.2). We conclude (Section 6.3) with some brief personal reflections on the evolution of our thinking about what may be productive approaches to future research and more theory-building on the role of written CF for L2 development.

6.1   A Summary of Theoretical Perspectives and Empirical Findings on Written CF

6.1.1   Cognitive perspectives

The cognitive approach to understanding how L2 learners develop their knowledge of and competence in using an L2 focuses on the mental processing of information about the L2 (referred to as input and as either positive evidence or negative evidence) and its use in the formulation of accurate and appropriate oral and written communication. In this book, our focus has been on a theoretical and empirical discussion of the potential of written CF (as explicit input) to facilitate L2 development, measured in terms of improved accuracy of output (the product), both immediately after the feedback has been provided and on subsequent occasions over time. The cognitive perspective not only claims that input, including written CF input, has the potential to facilitate L2 development in this way, but it also explains the conditions required for the effective processing of the feedback (Gass, 1997; Ortega, 2009) and social, individual and contextual factors/ variables that may interrupt a linear processing of the feedback (Ellis, 2010; Kormos, 2012). Written CF research, conducted within this perspective, has been less centred on an examination of the theoretical explanations than on more pedagogical questions of what approaches 'work best' (Polio, 2010). Thus, the empirical focus has tended to investigate the effect of written CF on improved/accurate output at various stages of use rather than on the actual processing of the information provided. Nevertheless, theoretical explanations have often been drawn upon in a number of studies to explain their findings.

6.1.1.1   Overview of the theoretical case

Drawing on theoretical claims and insights from the SLA literature, we presented a theoretical case or argument in Chapter 2 that can explain the contribution of written CF for L2 development. We explained that as a form of input, written CF has the potential to facilitate development if certain conditions are met. When learners receive explicit written CF input and consciously attend to it (Schmidt, 1990, 1994, 2001; Tomlin & Villa, 1994), the potential exists for them to notice that there is a mismatch between their output and the target language input provided in the written CF. If the learner does not notice with understanding, the process is unlikely to develop to the next stage identified in the information processing framework designed by Gass (1997), namely intake (Schmidt, 2001).

At both stages of the processing framework (attention and understanding), the type of written CF a learner receives may be a factor in determining whether or not it is understood. We suggested that learners with a more developed long-term memory store may need less explicit types of written CF to understand the feedback than those with a less developed long-term memory store. At the intake stage, we explained that learners need to be able to match the feedback with the knowledge already stored in their long-term memory. Because the matching process involves different levels of analysis and re-analysis in the working memory, learners with a greater working memory capacity may be able to consciously process a greater amount of information than learners with a more limited capacity (Ortega, 2009). In the process of comparing both sets of knowledge, the learner can make hypotheses about the correct modification required. Learners, for example, with a more developed long-term memory store, a greater working memory capacity and high levels of motivation may benefit as much from indirect types of written CF (that simply draw their attention to where an error has occurred) as from more explicit types of written CF (for example, direct CF and metalinguistic explanation). As each hypothesis is tested by means of a modification of the original output, any one of four outcomes is possible in the process of integration (the fourth stage of the framework): rejection, confirmation, storage, exiting the system (Gass, 1997). Accurately modified output is then an overt manifestation that the process of developing new explicit knowledge has begun. However, at any one of the five stages, the processing of the feedback may be derailed. Not only may the type of feedback provided impede the processing (for example, a type of feedback that is not comprehended by the learner), but a range of additional factors such those outlined in Chapter 2 (for example, social and individual factors) may moderate the process, positively or negatively (Kormos, 2012).

Once learners have successfully processed the written CF from an initial feedback episode and successfully modified their output, on-going opportunities to draw on their new knowledge when the same linguistic form or structure is required in new pieces of writing will enable them to consolidate what has been learnt (Housen & Pierrard, 2005; Williams, 2012). As skill acquisition theories explain, repeated retrievals of this explicit knowledge from their long-term memory, during meaningful practice, will provide them with opportunities for deeper processing, less controlled conscious processing and more proceduralised, automatic processing (Anderson, 1976, 1983, 1993; McLaughlin, 1978, 1987, 1990). Interface theorists argue that explicit knowledge can be converted to implicit knowledge through this consolidation process (DeKeyser, 1998; N. Ellis, 2005). Also, during this consolidation process, it is to be expected that learners will not always use their new knowledge with complete success and may need to receive further written CF when their output needs to be modified.

As we explained in Chapter 2, the provision of feedback in the written context may provide learners with advantages, less available in the oral context, for the processing stages summarised above. The permanence of the written text means that learners can refer back to the feedback they have received as often as they wish and can take as much time as they wish to think about the feedback they have received before attempting an accurate modification (Williams, 2012). These advantages mean that learners can take their time as they proceed through the five stages of the Gass (1997) framework, both initially and on subsequent occasions if further feedback is given during the consolidation phase.

6.1.1.2   Overview of the written CF research

To what extent, then, has the written CF research focused on a validation of this theoretical argument? In Chapter 3, we explained that most of the written CF studies have been more pedagogically framed than theoretically framed, and have given less attention to a validation of the processing referred to above. Nevertheless, the research has been of a theoretical nature insofar as it has investigated the potential for explicit feedback, in the form of written CF, to facilitate L2 learning and development, by measuring (in the form of pre-test/written CF treatment/post-test designs) the extent to which the product (namely, accurately modified output and accurate output in new pieces of writing) resulted from the feedback provided. We reported that this product-focused research (and therefore this pedagogically motivated research) underpinned the five overarching questions guiding the majority of studies.

Considering, first of all, the key question that any research on the contribution of written CF to L2 development needs to answer – whether or not written CF has the potential to facilitate L2 development – we reported the findings of an expanding research base, showing that learners who receive written CF (as opposed to those who don't) not only produce accurate revisions and accuracy in new texts immediately after the feedback has been provided, but often continue to do so on subsequent occasions over time (e.g. Bitchener & Knoch, 2010a, 2010b; Bitchener & Ferris, 2012; Sheen, 2007; Shintani & Ellis, 2013; Stefanou, 2014). However, as many commentators (e.g. Bitchener & Ferris, 2012; Shintani et al., 2014; Van Beunigen et al., 2012) are quick to point out, only a limited range of error categories have been tested so far, meaning that it would be premature to draw any firm conclusions about the generalizability of the findings to linguistic domains that are more complex and idiosyncratic than those investigated so far (that is, simple rule-based forms as opposed to those that are more complex or item-based).

The extent to which focused written CF (that is, the targeting of only one or a few error categories at a time) is more effective in producing accurate output than unfocused (more comprehensive) feedback is a question that has also been investigated but the limited number of studies that have compared the two approaches within a single research design means that no firm conclusions can yet be drawn even though the studies that have investigated only focused feedback have consistently shown that the approach is effective (see Bitchener & Ferris, 2012). It may be that there is a relationship between the linguistic focus of the feedback and the approach taken (that is, focused or unfocused). While an investigation into this relationship might explain, to some extent, the accuracy of output produced, it may also explain the extent to which the processing of the feedback is straightforward and linear.

The ubiquitous question about whether some types of written CF are more effective than other types, while pedagogically motivated in the early research, has more recently been considered from a theoretical perspective, namely, whether the degree of explicitness of each type of written CF has an effect on the output (the product) and the nature of the processing of the feedback. As we have shown, this product-focused research base has reported inconsistent findings. This is not altogether surprising given the range of design variables across the studies. As we have mentioned on a number of occasions in Chapter 3, any research question that seeks to find whether one type of written CF is more effective than a different type of written CF needs to control other variables, otherwise there is likely to be an interactional effect that may lead to different findings. The same research approach needs to be taken when comparing the relative effectiveness of other variables like, for example, focused and unfocused feedback interacting with different linguistic error categories. Additionally, it may be that different types of written CF alone, as well as different types of feedback, interacting with other variables, determine the nature of information processing from input to output. Other variables may include not only those that have been prominent in the research so far but also, and perhaps more significantly, those that have more recently been considered with regard to their effect on output, for example, individual processing capacity, analytic ability and the matching of knowledge in the long-term memory store with new knowledge from written CF in the learner's working memory.

Finally, we have reported the findings of a few studies (e.g. Bitchener & Knoch, 2008; Rummel, 2014; Sheen, 2007; Stefanou, 2014) that have investigated the effect of individual and contextual factors on the response of learners to written CF and its effect on output, but it has been noted that no firm conclusions can be drawn from the findings of so few studies. One would expect these factors to have an effect not only on the bookend stages of information processing (namely, attention to written CF input and output) but also on retrieval and processing during the consolidation phase, when learners (1) identify occasions when their new knowledge needs to be employed in the writing of new texts and (2) hypothesise the correct output required on each identified occasion.

In this section, we have summarised many of the key elements of the theoretical case presented in Chapter 2 – a case which explains (1) why written CF, as explicit input, has the potential to facilitate the development of new L2 knowledge (by means of cognitive information processing) and (2) how a range of individual and contextual factors may moderate cognitive processing at any of the stages. In Chapter 3, we discussed the extent to which the published written CF research has focused on (1) the processing of written CF input as opposed to its product (the output) and (2) the factors or variables that may facilitate or impede the effectiveness of written CF for L2 development.

6.1.2   Sociocultural perspectives

Sociocultural theory views written CF from a different vantage point to that adopted by cognitive perspectives. Although SCT views written CF as important for L2 development, it focuses on answering the question of **why** written CF may or may not be effective. What distinguishes SCT from cognitive theories is that, in order to answer this question, SCT does not consider the working of the human brain (e.g. long-term memory, hypothesis testing) but rather the quality of the feedback provided in relation to the individual learner's evolving capacities (ZPD), how the feedback is processed as a form of problem-solving activity (languaging), how it is delivered (tools), and in particular the personal, interpersonal and context-specific dimensions of the feedback as an activity. Unlike the large and growing body of research on written CF informed by cognitive theories of SLA, research informed by SCT is to date quite modest in size and in scale.

As discussed in Chapter 4, from a sociocultural theoretical perspective, written CF is a form of assistance made available in social interaction between an expert and a novice (or a group of novices). However, SCT also stipulates that not all forms of assistance are effective for cognitive development. For assistance to be effective it must be co-constructed between the expert and the novice so that it is graduated and contingently responsive to the novice's existing and potential capacities (ZPD), ultimately enabling the novice to function independently. The metaphor used to describe this kind of developmental and dynamic assistance is scaffolding. Thus, in terms of written CF, SCT claims that for feedback to be conducive to L2 learning, it needs to be carefully attuned to the individual learner's ability to understand the feedback and to take advantage of it. At the same time, it needs to push learners to perform at their potential rather than their present level of L2 capacities. Too much feedback or too much explicit feedback may be ineffective because it may not encourage the learner to become self-regulated, ultimately assuming responsibility for the accuracy of their texts. To reiterate, the claim made by SCT is that written CF is of paramount importance for L2 development because it is a form of assistance, but that it will only be effective to the extent that it is scaffolded, taking into consideration the learner's evolving ZPD. Such assistance enables the learner to apply knowledge internalised during the interaction to novel situations.

Empirical research investigating this claim, as detailed in Chapter 5, has focused on feedback provided by teachers in oral conferences (e.g. Aljaafreh & Lantolf, 1994; Nassaji & Swain, 2000) and by peers in peer response activities (e.g. Guerrero & Villamil, 2000) or in collaborative writing tasks (e.g. Brooks & Swain, 2009). These studies suggest that when the teacher provides scaffolded feedback, attuned to the learner's ZPD, this is more beneficial than non-scaffolded or random feedback and that peers can provide each other with scaffolded feedback or engage in collective scaffolding. However, what is absent in most of these studies is evidence that knowledge co-constructed during interaction has been internalised, and that the learner can independently use this internalised knowledge when composing new texts. Other limitations of research on scaffolded CF include the fact that this research has investigated mainly feedback delivered in one-on-one conferences and that most of this research has been conducted with ESL learners.

We noted in Chapter 4 that SCT also attributes much importance to mediational tools in cognitive development. Tools, whether symbolic or material, enhance and shape our actions, including our thinking processes. In the provision and processing of feedback, it is generally language, a symbolic tool, which enables the communication and the co-construction of the feedback, as well as the processing and internalisation of the feedback. Language enables learners to form abstract mental representations of linguistic information previously made available in external forms (via written or oral feedback comments), and to reflect on that knowledge.

Research has suggested a correlation between deliberations about language (languaging) and revisions. Studies have shown that when learners deliberate (i.e. language) about the feedback they receive, whether orally with a peer (e.g. Storch & Wigglesworth, 2010a) or with the feedback provider (e.g. Tocalli-Beller & Swain, 2005), or on their own (in written languaging, see Suzuki, 2012), this results in improved performance on revised drafts. These findings suggest that the extent to which written CF is effective depends also on whether learners engage actively with the feedback provided. However, what has not been investigated is whether languaging encourages the internalisation of what has been languaged about, and the transfer of this knowledge to new writing; that is, whether languaging about the information provided in the feedback results in L2 development.

Material tools used to provide feedback may also affect learners' engagement with written CF. Research comparing computer-mediated feedback provided by teachers and even more so by peers with traditional forms of written CF suggests that computer-mediated feedback may affect the quantity and quality of the corrective feedback provided (e.g. Liu & Sadler, 2003) as well as the quality of learners' engagement with the feedback (e.g. Chang, 2012; Guardado & Shi, 2007). To date, most of this research has been descriptive and not always well designed, reporting on the impact of the various tools on revisions rather than on new writing.

The other distinguishing feature of SCT, and specifically activity theory (AT), is its attempt to explain human behaviour and the outcome of that behaviour by using activity and its interacting elements as its unit of analysis. AT provides researchers with an analytical framework that can be used to analyse and interpret human behaviour in a particular context and when engaging in a particular activity such as language learning. In the case of written corrective feedback, AT, by examining the personal, interpersonal and context-specific dimensions of the activity, can help explain why written CF may or may not lead to L2 development. From this perspective, the participants (students and teachers) are viewed as active agents, who come into the activity with their own goals, beliefs and preferences. As Hyland and Hyland (2006a: 220) point out, students are not passive recipients of written CF, but rather 'active agents who respond to what they see as valuable and useful and to people they regard as engaging and credible'. Teachers, too, are active agents, and their feedback practices may be governed not only by their own pedagogical beliefs, and the goals they wish to achieve, but also by the identity they wish to portray. Furthermore, feedback is a situated activity, and thus the kind of feedback provided and the response to that feedback may also be shaped by cultural and institutional norms and expectations. Viewing the provision and students' response to written CF as an activity extends our analysis and consequently our understanding of why corrective feedback may or may not be effective in the case of a particular learner or indeed an entire class of learners (e.g. Lee, 2014).

As noted in Chapter 5, despite its potential usefulness, AT has not been utilised to a great extent by L2 researchers investigating written CF. Although some researchers have alluded to some elements of the theory when explaining learners' response to feedback (e.g. Hyland, 1998; Storch & Wigglesworth, 2010a, 2010b), teacher feedback practices (e.g. Lee, 2008b) or to notions of learner agency, the use of the entire model of AT is rare in L2 research on written CF. Lee (2014) employed the second generation (G_2) of the model retrospectively to map findings from her earlier (2008a, 2008b) studies, and Thorne (2004) used it to investigate a peer response activity. The fact that this theory is seldom used in studies on feedback is perhaps not surprising given the complexity of the theory and some of the confusion surrounding the terms used (e.g. object/motive/goal). Conceptualising learners' responses and feedback practices as interrelated activity systems (G_3 of the model) may be particularly challenging for researchers.

6.2   Future Directions

In this section, we outline the kind of research we would do well to focus on in future investigations of written CF. We discuss the kind of research that can strengthen, confirm or clarify the claims made by cognitive explanations and by sociocultural perspectives regarding the contribution of written CF to L2 development. We also consider areas of both cognitive and sociocultural theory that we believe would benefit from further theorising.

6.2.1   Cognitive perspectives

In Chapter 2, we presented an argued case in support of the view that when written CF (as explicit input) is made available to the learner, it has the potential to be consciously used to produce accurate output and, thus, set in motion the process of L2 development. Interface theorists claim that this explicit knowledge can then be converted to implicit knowledge as it becomes more proceduralised and automatised over time. The argument presented has drawn upon a range of theoretical claims and hypotheses, most typically considered in relation to L2 learning/acquisition as it occurs in oral interactional contexts. Insofar as this is the first occasion on which an overall theoretical case has been published to explain how and why explicit written input (in the form of written CF) may contribute to L2 development, further work is needed, on the theoretical level, to account for the potentially moderating effect of both cognitive and non-cognitive factors/variables on a learner's response to cognitive processing of and use of written CF in revised and new pieces of writing. Theory-building such as this is important if we are to understand how and why written CF may facilitate L2 development and set relevant research agendas.

To date, little attention has been given to examining the extent to which the proposed theoretical arguments offer valid explanations of how and why written CF may facilitate L2 development. Essentially, the research has investigated whether or not written CF can result in more accurate output and whether or not certain variables/factors might facilitate or impede the production of accurate output (for example, pedagogical factors like type of written CF that is provided and the linguistic focus of the feedback, social and contextual factors and individual cognitive and affective factors). Until recently, little attention has been given to the potential impact of these factors on how learners respond to written CF and on the nature of their conscious processing of the information provided. We offer, therefore, the following recommendations for further written CF research, starting with those that might usefully develop our current understanding of insights on the **output or product** arising from written CF (Section 6.2.1.1) and concluding with those that might aid our understanding of how learners **respond to, process and use** the feedback (Section 6.2.1.2).

6.2.1.1   Focus on output (the product)

One of our often-repeated refrains in Chapter 3 was the need for more research on questions that have so far failed to produce consistent findings on the effectiveness of written CF. We explained that consistent findings could only be obtained if variables across studies are held constant. To this end, approximate replication studies would be the most effective type of study because they seek to reduce the number of design variables.

We also explained that most of the available studies sought answers to questions about whether one written CF approach (for example, one type of written CF) can be expected to be more effective than others in producing more accurate output. The dearth of consistent findings across studies on such questions (for example, whether metalinguistic explanation is more effective than direct error correction) makes it clear that further research would be better to focus on examining the potentially complex interaction of variables so that firmer conclusions can be drawn about the conditions and circumstances under which effectiveness might be expected. Such conditions might include the linguistic focus of the feedback, the proficiency level of the learner (meaning, for example, the size of the learner's long-term memory store and working memory capacity) and individual factors (for example, beliefs about written CF, motivation and so on). The findings of replication studies and those that consider a range of interacting factors might then be compared with existing studies where the same or similar factors/variables are present.

For the most part, studies to date have tended to examine the effect of only a single written CF treatment. Consequently, we do not know whether learners in cross-sectional studies who failed to improve the accuracy of their written output after receiving written CF might have benefited if written CF had been provided on more than one occasion. It may be that only one additional feedback episode (for example, with the same types of feedback or with a more explicit type) is required to set the learner on a developmental path. Research that investigates these possibilities should be a part of future research agendas.

6.2.1.2   Focus on response, processing and use

Further research should not only focus on the output/product but also, and arguably more importantly, on how and why learners respond to written CF, how they cognitively process it and how they use it in revised and new pieces of writing. Studies that seek to understand the processing stages of both a single written CF episode and recurrent episodes during the on-going consolidation phase will help us not only understand what is required for accurate output but also why learners might fail to benefit from its provision and at which stage the processing may be more likely to break down. Studies that adopt these aims will need to be more longitudinal and include a wider range of data sources (for example, questionnaire, interview, think aloud, stimulated recall) as well as delayed post-test pieces of writing. Additionally, studies that focus on processing would do well to investigate the extent to which individual cognitive and non-cognitive factors, as well as contextual factors (including pedagogical approaches/factors) may impact on the processing of written CF episodes (both immediately and over time). Studies that adopt these aims will begin to meet the call for research that is more theoretically motivated, that is, research that is more focused on understanding how and why written CF can be expected to play a positive role in L2 development.

Perhaps the most difficult theoretical research question to investigate is that which focuses on whether the explicit knowledge that learners understand and use accurately is converted to implicit knowledge and used automatically without recourse to conscious processing. The vexed questions of how to measure implicit knowledge and determine whether, in fact, a learner has drawn upon implicit knowledge rather than explicit knowledge when producing accurate written output are clearly important to theorists but possibly less important to classroom practitioners. Nevertheless, future research should try to grapple with these questions and seek ways to investigate them. In recent times, it has been proposed that written CF might be more advantageous than oral CF for L2 development. It is certainly an interesting question but probably one that is likely to be more usefully investigated if it includes an examination of the conditions upon which written and oral CF are most beneficial.

6.2.2   Sociocultural perspectives

Sociocultural theory views development of higher order cognitive capacities, including competence in using an L2, as occurring in interaction (not as a result of interaction). Development is viewed as a socialisation process (akin to socialising children to become independent members of society) and thus the focus of the theory is on understanding human social interaction, between an expert and novice members of the society. In the L2 learning context, the expert may be a teacher or a peer who provides appropriate assistance to the L2 learner. The theory claims that for that assistance to be effective it needs to be co-constructed between the expert and learner, so that it is attuned and responsive to the evolving needs of the learner (scaffolded). Only such assistance will enable the learner to perform at his/her potential rather than existing capacity (ZPD) and result in development. It is also important to note that development from this perspective is evident not only in independent performance (greater accuracy on new texts) but also in a reduced reliance on assistance (from the expert or more explicit forms of feedback). Thus, SCT justifies written CF for L2 development by seeing it as a form of assistance. However, because only effective assistance is facilitative of development, SCT identifies the traits of effective feedback. In this book, we described these traits of effective written CF and presented limited research findings, which suggest that carefully scaffolded feedback is more effective than random feedback.

We noted that SCT does not have much to say about the mental processing of the feedback provided, apart from suggesting that internalisation means that knowledge co-constructed during interaction becomes a resource that the learner can draw on in independent activity.

A distinguishing feature of SCT is the important role it attributes to mediational tools, be they symbolic (e.g. language) or material (e.g. computers). These tools enable action to take place but also shape the action. For example, material tools may affect not only the nature of the feedback provided (e.g. the quantity of feedback when provided by computers) but also on the quality of learners' engagement with the feedback. Language, the symbolic tool, enables not only feedback to be provided, but also for learners to process feedback and to deliberate about it (e.g. question the feedback, self-directed explanations). Studies investigating the role of tools suggest that the quality of the engagement may impact on whether the feedback will be internalised, although to date these studies have investigated the impact of these mediational tools on the ability to revise rather than ability to use the internalised knowledge in independent new writing.

Perhaps the greatest contribution that SCT and more specifically AT make to our understanding of written CF is in its systematic and comprehensive view of what are referred to as learner (e.g. goals, previous educational experience) and context-related variables (e.g. expected norms of behaviour). By viewing the learner as an intentional agent acting within a specific context, the theory helps explain why feedback provided to one learner or group of learners in a particular context may or may not lead to L2 development. The aim of this body of research is not only to explain the outcome but also to help identify aspects of the activity that need modification.

As mentioned previously, research informed by SCT is modest and small scale. Evidence of L2 development has been, for the most part, restricted to learners' abilities to incorporate written CF in revised drafts or to self-correct. We thus need not only more studies and of a larger scale (beyond a few case studies), but also better designed studies; specifically, future studies guided by SCT need to include pre-and post-tests or new pieces of writing to provide more convincing evidence of L2 development.

In the following sections, we suggest some areas for further investigation and offer some advice on how this research could be implemented.

6.2.2.1   Scaffolding

Given the importance that SCT attributes to scaffolded feedback for L2 development, and the limited number of studies that have investigated and compared the outcomes of scaffolded and unscaffolded feedback, clearly much more research is needed on the benefits of written CF that is scaffolded. Furthermore, in most of the studies that investigated the impact of scaffolded feedback (e.g. Aljaafreh & Lantolf, 1994) or compared scaffolded and unscaffolded feedback (e.g. Nassaji & Swain, 2000), the feedback was provided in oral conferences. This is not surprising given that scaffolding needs to be tailored to individual learner needs, and this is more easily achieved in one-on-one conferences where the feedback is dialogic and hence more amenable to continuous fine-tuning. The provision of individually tailored feedback creates something of a challenge for teachers as well as a challenge for researchers who want to extend the scope of the investigations into scaffolded feedback.

However, developments in the design of computer-delivered dynamic assessment outlined by Poehner and Lantolf (2010) may address this challenge. The system the researchers developed employs a pre-fabricated menu of five graduated hints, arranged on a scale from implicit to explicit. The response to an error is initially implicit, but gradually becomes more explicit with successive incorrect attempts. The final hint provides the correct response with a metalinguistic explanation. The greatest drawback of this system is that it lacks the fine-grained tuning available during dialogic interaction. However, the advantage of this interventionist system, especially if delivered in a computerised format, is that it can be provided to large cohorts of learners. Future studies need to investigate the efficacy of this computerised scaffolded written CF.

Furthermore, we need studies which examine the nature of written CF provided on successive written drafts, on whether that feedback shows traits of scaffolding which takes the learner's ability to respond to feedback on earlier drafts into consideration, and indeed whether scaffolded written CF results in L2 development as evident in more accurately produced texts. This research can perhaps be most easily implemented as retrospective action research, in writing classes that adopt a process approach to L2 writing instruction, or in graduate writing programmes where multiple drafts are a common practice. Given the growing number of graduate students who are writing their dissertations in their additional language (predominantly ESL), studies examining the feedback given by supervisors on successive drafts and what use students make of this feedback and why are very timely.

Research on scaffolded written CF conducted in a range of contexts, with different cohorts of students can help substantiate claims made by SCT about the importance of scaffolding. It can also inform teacher and supervisor feedback practices.

6.2.2.2 Mediational tools

SCT highlights the importance of mediating tools, whether symbolic or material, in how learners process and engage with written CF. Extant research is limited and has considered mainly what impact tools have on learners' engagement with feedback, and, to a lesser extent, how the nature of the processing affects revisions. Clearly we need research that examines how engagement with feedback affects L2 development, measured by performance on new writing.

For example, one important area to investigate is the impact of the use of language, a symbolic tool in deliberations (languaging) about feedback and whether these deliberations, and the quality of these deliberations, ultimately have an impact on L2 development. Studies pursuing this line of research will need to collect data on the quality of languaging episodes (in oral or written form) and then trace the use of the language structures, which were deliberated about in the languaging episodes, in new pieces of writing. This line of research, however, requires the use of tailor-made pair or individual tests, as we cannot predict what learners will choose to pay attention to in their languaging. Such research could inform us whether the quality of languaging has a bearing on L2 development, helping to answer the question of whether intensive deliberations about the use of a structure lead to the ability to use the structure in future writing more so than superficial deliberations. The close link between depth of noticing of written CF, understanding the feedback, and L2 development is a claim also made in cognitive theories of SLA (e.g. Schmidt, 2001), yet it is one which is relatively unexplored in empirical research on written CF. Furthermore, given that L2 learners have at their disposal more than one language, another interesting and related area of research is to examine which language (L1 or L2) advanced L2 learners use when processing feedback, and the impact of the choice of language may have on processing the written CF.

With rapid technological advancements and the deployment of computer-mediated means of providing and communicating about written CF in online courses and distance supervision arrangements, an important area for future research is also how these new material tools affect the nature of the feedback provided and learners' response to and internalisation of that feedback. In particular, recent research attention has focused on the language learning potential of feedback provided by automated writing evaluation software. According to Stevenson and Phakiti (2014), these commercially available programmes (e.g. Criterion, QBL) are increasingly being used in writing classrooms for formative assessment purposes across the educational spectrum in the USA. In their critical review of studies investigating the effects of automated feedback programmes on learners' texts, Stevenson and Phakiti concluded that, as yet, it is difficult to conclude whether automated feedback is effective. What has hampered their ability to draw firmer conclusions is the limited number of studies, contradictory findings in published studies, and the flaws in the design of existing research including the lack of new writing.

Thus what we need is well-designed studies on computer-mediated written CF, including automated feedback, which examine the nature of the feedback provided, how learners engage with that feedback, and its impact on learners' ability to develop more independent self-editing skills as well as produce more accurate texts. Such studies will have important implications for the design of these tools as well as for pedagogy. For example, they can inform teachers how these tools could be used for optimal effect (e.g. in combination with face-to-face conferences).

6.2.2.3   Activity theory

To date, the limited research on factors that may explain why corrective feedback is effective or not in the case of individual learners has tended to focus on one variable at a time (see discussion in Kormos, 2012). Activity theory (AT) provides researchers with a theoretical heuristic, a heuristic that enables researchers to see how individual and contextual variables relate to and influence each other when investigating human activity. If we view written CF as an activity, including the provision and response to feedback, in order to fully understand why the feedback is beneficial or not for L2 development, we need longitudinal, classroom-based studies (see argument in Storch, 2010b) which investigate how and why learners engage with the feedback and feedback providers. Such studies need to provide readers with a comprehensive description of the context in which the feedback is given and used (e.g. the importance attributed to accuracy, assessment practices, institutional policies), and about the participants in the feedback activity (e.g. their goals, expectations, language learning histories).

Employing an AT framework in research on written CF has implications for data collection tools and the type of data collected. Surveys and students' written texts (students' drafts with feedback, revised drafts and new writing) provide only part of the story. Texts may not explain why students respond to the corrective feedback in a particular way. Rather, we need multiple sources of data that could inform us about the broader context as well as the immediate context. Such data could include interviews with stake holders, educational policy documents, observations of classes in which the feedback activity takes place, and interviews with the participants that could shed light on the participants (students and teachers), relationships, goals and expectations. Such data tends to be qualitative and requires triangulation. Mapping this data onto the second (G_2) or third (G_3) generation of AT models (described in Chapter 4 and its application illustrated in Chapter 5) enables the researcher to consider these factors simultaneously which may in turn help in explaining the outcomes of the feedback activity. Furthermore, and as shown by the few studies that have employed AT to analyse written CF (e.g. Lee, 2014), such research can be used to identify the sources of tensions and weaknesses in the feedback activity and enable researchers to recommend appropriate innovations.

6.3   Final Reflections

We would like to conclude with some insights we gained in authoring individual chapters and in co-authoring this book, when we as authors reflected on what we read and wrote and as co-authors when we read and engaged with each other's contributions. We began, as evident in the structure of the book, by presenting the two major theoretical paradigms, cognitive and sociocultural, which provide different perspectives on L2 learning and different approaches to investigate written CF. However, in the process of writing the book, we realised that the two paradigms may, in fact, provide complementary insights on written CF on L2 writing. We would thus like to encourage future researchers to consider how both theoretical perspectives can inform and complement each other.

We have seen in this book that explanations informed by cognitive perspectives focus on the potential of written CF to facilitate L2 development if learners attend to and consciously process the information they are given (through the information processing stages previously discussed in Chapter 2) to the point where they hypothesise and produce an accurate and appropriate modification of the targeted linguistic error. These perspectives also explain that, at any point in these stages, individual (cognitive and affective) and contextual (social and pedagogical) factors may facilitate or impede the progression from one stage of processing to another. This may not only occur during the initial written CF episode but also at any stage of information retrieval or when further processing of ongoing written CF during the consolidation phase of development is required. As we have shown, considerable attention has been given to investigating whether or not some pedagogical options (direct and indirect CF, metalinguistic explanation, focused and unfocused written CF) may be more effective in facilitating L2 development than others, but less attention has been given to the potentially moderating effect of these options on attention and information processing. Most recently, researchers have started to investigate the potential of individual factors (cognitive and affective) to moderate progress at any of the stages referred to above. While the findings from these research initiatives are beginning to indicate the extent to which written CF can contribute to L2 development, the directions for further research (discussed earlier in this chapter as well as in Chapters 3 and 5) will need to be considered if the field is to move forward in any systematic and transformational way.

SCT views interaction as the cornerstone of all cognitive development, with an expert providing the novice with appropriate assistance that will result in development. Written CF is a form of assistance provided by an expert (teacher or more able peer), that if finely tuned to the needs of the learner has the potential to be internalised and lead to L2 development. Development is viewed as a gradual process of decreasing dependence not only on the expert but also on concrete representations of knowledge (e.g. grammar rules). The novice learner is considered independent (self-regulated) when he or she can write accurate texts independently, drawing on abstract representations of grammatical knowledge. What SCT and AT highlight is the potential impact of mediational tools, both symbolic (e.g. language) and material tools (e.g. computers), of individual learner, and of context-specific dimensions on how learners engage with the assistance (process-written CF) and whether they accept and internalise it. These dimensions are encapsulated in the theory of activity.

However, as we mentioned earlier, what SCT does not explain very clearly is the internalisation process. How does scaffolded knowledge become part of the learner's unique resources that the learner can deploy in independent activity? This is perhaps the area of SCT that requires further development. For this reason, research informed by SCT and by AT perspectives may be best equipped to explain why CF was or was not effective for a particular learner or group of learners but not how it was internalised. These explanations could include, for example, whether and why the learner, as a volitional agent, chooses to notice and engage with the feedback, what impact the means of providing the feedback or the person who provided the feedback had on learner's response to and engagement with the feedback, and finally other context and participant-specific dimensions that may explain the feedback activity.

We believe that research that draws on both theoretical perspectives can expand our understanding of how written CF can contribute more effectively to L2 development. Such research may be of potential interest not only to L2 researchers but also to L2 teachers. As Lantolf and Thorne (2006) argue, research needs to be transformational. The task for researchers is not merely to describe and analyse a corrective feedback activity, but to transform and improve it. We look forward to reading theoretically driven and informed studies that pursue some of the research directions we have outlined.

References

AbuSeileek, A. (2013) Using track changes and word processor to provide corrective feedback to learners in writing. *Journal of Computer Assisted Learning* 29, 319–333.

AbuSeileek, A. and Abualsha'r, A. (2014) Using peer computer-mediated corrective feedback to support EFL learners' writing. *Language Learning & Technology* 18 (1), 76–95.

Adams, R. (2003) L2 output, reformulation and noticing: Implications for IL development. *Language Teaching Research* 7, 347–376.

Al Shahrani, A. and Storch, N. (2014) Investigating teachers' written corrective feedback practices in a Saudi EFL context: How do they align with their beliefs, institutional guidelines, and students' preferences? *Australian Review of Applied Linguistics* 37, 101–122.

Aljaafreh, A. and Lantolf, J.P. (1994) Negative feedback as regulation and second language learning in the zone of proximal development. *Modern Language Journal* 78, 465–483.

Amrhein, H.R. and Nassaji, H. (2008) Written corrective feedback: What do students and teachers prefer and why? *Canadian Journal of Applied Linguistics* 29 (3), 456–482.

Anderson, J. (1976) *Language, Memory, and Thought*. Hillsdale, NJ: lawrence Erlbaum.

Anderson, J. (1980) *Cognitive Psychology and its Implications*. Cambridge, MA: Harvard University Press.

Anderson, J. (1983) *The Architecture of Cognition*. Cambridge, MA: Harvard University Press.

Anderson, J. (1993) *Rules of the Mind*. Hillsdale, NJ: Lawrence Erlbaum.

Ashwell, T. (2000) Patterns of teacher response to student writing in a multiple-draft composition classroom: Is content feedback followed by form feedback the best method? *Journal of Second Language Writing* 9 (3), 227–257.

Bandura, A. (1997) *Self-efficacy: The Exercise of Control*. New York: W.H. Freeman.

Basturkmen, H. East, M. and Bitchener, J. (2014) Supervisors' on-script feedback comments on drafts of dissertations: Socialising students into the academic discourse community. *Teaching in Higher Education* 19 (4), 432–445.

Benesch, S. (2012) *Considering Emotions in Critical English Language Teaching: Theories and praxis*. New York and London: Routledge.

Bitchener, J. (2008) Evidence in support of written corrective feedback. *Journal of Second Language Writing* 17 (2), 102–118.

Bitchener, J. (2009) Measuring the effectiveness of written corrective feedback: A response to 'Overgeneralization from a narrow focus: A response to Bitchener (2008)'. *Journal of Second Language Writing* 18 (4), 276–279.

Bitchener, J. (2012) A reflection on 'the language learning potential' of written CF. *Journal of Second Language Writing* 21, 348–363.

Bitchener, J. and Ferris, D. (2012) *Written Corrective Feedback in Second Language Acquisition and Writing*. London: Routledge.

Bitchener, J. and Knoch, U. (2008) The value of written corrective feedback for migrant and international students. *Language Teaching Research* 12 (3), 409–431.

Bitchener, J. and Knoch, U. (2009a) The value of a focused approach to written corrective feedback. *ELT Journal* 63 (3), 204–211.

Bitchener, J. and Knoch, U. (2009b) The relative effectiveness of different types of direct written corrective feedback. *System* 37 (2), 322–329.

Bitchener, J. and Knoch, U. (2010a) The contribution of written corrective feedback to language development: A ten month investigation. *Applied Linguistics* 31 (2), 193–214.

Bitchener, J. and Knoch, U. (2010b) Raising the linguistic accuracy level of advanced L2 writers with written corrective feedback. *Journal of Second Language Writing* 19 (4), 207–217.

Bitchener, J. Basturkmen, H. and East, M. (2010) The focus of supervisors written feedback to disser/dissertation students. *International Journal of English Studies* 10 (2), 79–99.

Bitchener, J., Young, S. and Cameron, D. (2005) The effect of different types of corrective feedback on ESL student writing. *Journal of Second Language Writing* 14 (3), 191–205.

Bodker, S. (1997) Computers in mediated human activity. *Mind, Culture and Activity: An International Journal* 4, 149–158.

Brooks, L. and Swain, M. (2009) Languaging in collaborative writing: Creation and response to expertise. In A. Mackey and C. Polio (eds) *Multiple Perspectives on Interaction in SLA* (pp. 58–89). Mahwah, NJ: Lawrence Erlbaum

Bruton, A. (2009) Designing research into the effect of error correction in L2 writing: Not so straightforward. *Journal of Second Language Writing* 18 (2), 136–140.

Carroll, J. (1981) Twenty-five years of research on foreign language aptitude. In K. Diller (ed.) *Individual Differences and Universals in Language Learning Aptitude* (pp. 83–118). Rowley, MA: Newbury House.

Celce-Murcia, M., Larsen-Freeman, D. and Williams, H.A. (1999) The grammar book: An ESL/EFL teacher's course (2nd edn). Massachusetts: Newbury House Rowley.

Chandler, J. (2003) The efficacy of various kinds of error feedback for improvement in the accuracy and fluency of L2 student writing. *Journal of Second Language Writing* 12 (3), 267–296.

Chang, C-F. (2012) Peer review via three modes in an EFL writing course. *Computers and Composition* 29 (1), 63–78.

Centeno-Cortés, B. and Jiménez-Jiménez, A. (2004) Problem-solving tasks in a foreign language: The importance of the L1 in private verbal thinking. *International Journal of Applied Linguistics* 14, 7–35.

Connor, U. and Asenavage, K. (1994) Peer response groups in ESL writing classes: How much impact on revision? *Journal of Second Language Writing* 3, 257–276.

Coughlan, P. and Duff, P. (1994) Same task, different activities: Analysis of SLA task from an activity theory perspective. In J.P. Lantolf and G. Appel (eds) *Vygotskian Approaches to Second Language Research* (pp. 173–191). Norwood, NJ: Ablex.

Davis, K.A. (1995) Qualitative theory and methods in applied linguistics research. *TESOL Quarterly* 29 (3), 427–453.

Deci, E.L. and Ryan, R.M. (1985) *Intrinsic Motivation and Self-determination in Human Behaviour.* New York: Plenum.

Dekeyser, R.M. (1997) Beyond explicit rule learning: Automatizing second language morphosyntax. *Studies in Second Language Acquisition* 19, 195–221.

Dekeyser. R.M. (1998) Beyond focus on form: Cognitive perspectives on learning and practising second language grammar. In C. Doughty and J. Williams (eds) *Focus on Form in Classroom Second Language Acquisition.* Cambridge: Cambridge University Press.

Dekeyser, R.M. (2003) Implicit and explicit learning. In C. Doughty and M.H. Long (eds) *The Hand Book of Second Language Acquisition* (pp. 313–348). Oxford: Blackwell publishing.

Dekeyser, R.M. (2007) Introduction: Situating the concept of practice. In R. Dekeyser (ed.) *Practice in a Second Language.* Cambridge: Cambridge University Press.

Donato, R. (1994) Collective scaffolding in second language learning. In J.P. Lantolf and G. Appel (eds) *Vygotskian Approaches to Second Language Research* (pp. 33–56). Norwood, NJ: Ablex.

Dörnyei, Z. (2001) *Motivational Strategies in the Language Classroom.* Cambridge: Cambridge University Press.

Dörnyei, Z. (2005) *The Psychology of the Language Learner*. US: Lawrence Erlbaum Associates.

Dörnyei, Z. (2010) The relationship between language aptitude and language learning motivation. In E. Macaro (ed.) *Continuum Companion to Second Language Acquisition* (pp. 247–267). London: Continuum.

Dornyei, Z. and Ushioda, E. (eds) (2009) *Motivation, Language Identity and the L2 Self*. Bristol: Multilingual Matters.

Ellis, N.C. (2005) At the interface: How explicit knowledge affects implicit language learning. *Studies in Second Language Acquisition* 27, 305–352.

Ellis, R. (2008) *The Study of Second Language Acquisition* (2nd edn). New York: Oxford University Press.

Ellis, R. (2009) A typology of written corrective feedback types. *ELT Journal* 63 (2), 97–107.

Ellis, R. (2010) Cognitive, social, and psychological dimensions corrective feedback. In R. Batstone (ed.) *Sociocognitive Perspectives on Language Use and Language Learning* (pp. 151–165). Oxford: Oxford University Press.

Ellis, R., Loewen, S. and Erlam, R. (2006) Implicit and explicit corrective feedback and the acquisition of L2 grammar. *Studies in Second Language Acquisition* 28 (2), 339–368.

Ellis, R., Sheen, Y., Murakami, M. and Takashima, H. (2008) The effects of focused and unfocused written corrective feedback in an English as a foreign language context. *System* 36 (3), 353–371.

Engeström, Y. (1987) *Learning by Expanding: An Activity-theoretical Approach to Developmental Research*. Helsinki: Orienta-Konsultit Oy.

Engeström, Y. (2001) Expansive learning at work: Toward an activity theoretical reconceptualization. *Journal of Education and Work* 14, 133–156.

Erlam, R., Ellis, R. and Batstone, R. (2013) Oral corrective feedback on L2 writing: Two approaches compared. *System* 41, 257–268.

Evans, N., Hartshorn, J. and Tuioti, E. (2010) Written corrective feedback: Practitioners' perspectives. *International Journal of English Studies* 10 (2), 47–77.

Fathman, A.K. and Whalley, E. (1990) Teacher response to student writing: focus on form versus content. In B. Kroll (ed.) *Second Language Writing* (pp. 178–190). Cambridge: Cambridge University Press.

Ferris, D. (1999) The case for grammar correction in L2 writing classes: A response to Truscott (1996) *Journal of Second Language Writing* 8 (1), 1–11.

Ferris, D. (2002) *Treatment of Error in Second Language Writing*. AnnArbor, MI: University of Michigan Press.

Ferris, D. (2003) *Response to Student Writing: Implications for Second Language Students*. Mahwah, NJ: Lawrence Erlbaum Associates.

Ferris, D. (2004) The 'grammar correction' debate in L2 writing: Where are we, and where do we go from here? (and what do we do in the meantime...?) *Journal of Second Language Writing* 13, 49–62.

Ferris, D. (2010) Second language writing research and written corrective feedback in SLA: Intersections and practical applications. *Studies in Second Language Acquisition* 32, 181–201.

Ferris, D. (2014) Responding to student writing: Teachers' philosophies and practices. *Assessing Writing* 19 (1), 6–23.

Ferris, D. and Roberts, B. (2001) Error feedback in L2 writing classes: How explicit does it need to be? *Journal of Second Language Writing* 10 (3), 161–184.

Frawley, W. and Lantolf, J. (1985) Second language discourse: A Vygotskyan perspective. *Applied Linguistics* 6 (1), 19–44.

Frear, D. (2012) The Effect of Written CF and Revision on Intermediate Chinese Learners' Acquisition of English. Unpublished doctoral thesis, University of Auckland, New Zealand.

Feuerstein, R., Rand, Y. and Hoffman, M. (1979) The dynamic assessment of retarded performers: The learning potential assessment device. *Theory, Instruments, and Techniques.* Baltimore, MD: University Park Press.

Feuerstein, R., Rand, Y. and Rynders, M. (1988) *Don't Accept Me as I am. Helping Retarded Performers Excel.* New York: Plenum.

Gardner, R.C. (1985) *Social Psychology and Second Language Learning: The Role of Attitudes and Motivation.* London: Edward Arnold.

Gardner, R.C. (2006) The socio-educational model of second language acquisition: A research paradigm. *EUROSLA Yearbook 6,* 237–260.

Gass, S. (1997) *Input, Interaction, and the Second Language Learner.* Mahwah, NJ: Lawrence Erlbaum Associates.

Gass, S. and Mackey, A. (2000) *Stimulated Recall Methodology in Second Language Research.* Mahwah, NJ: Lawrence Erlbaum Associates.

Goldstein, L. (2001) For Kyla: What does the research say about responding to ESL writers? In T. Silva and P. Matsuda (eds) *On Second Language Writing* (pp. 73–90). Mahwah, NJ: Lawrence Erlbaum Associates.

Goldstein, L. (2004) Questions and answers about teacher written commentary and student revision: Teachers and students working together. *Journal of Second Language Writing* 13 (1), 63–80.

Goldstein, L.M. (2006) Feedback and revision in second language writing: Contextual, teacher, and student variables. In K. Hyland and F. Hyland (eds) *Feedback in Second Language Writing: Contexts and issues* (pp. 185–205). Cambridge, England: Cambridge University Press.

Goo, J. and Mackey, A. (2013) The case against the case against recasts. *Studies in Second Language Acquisition* 35, 127–165.

Granott, N. (2005) Scaffolding dynamically toward change: Previous and new perspectives. *New Ideas in Psychology* 23, 140–151.

Guardado, M. and Shi, L. (2007) ESL students' experiences of online peer feedback. *Computers and Composition* 24 (4), 443–461

Guenette, D. (2007) Is feedback pedagogically correct? Research design issues in studies of feedback in writing. *Journal of Second Language Writing* 16 (1), 40–53.

Guerrero, M.C.M. de and Villamil, O.S. (1994) Social-cognitive dimensions of interaction in L2 peer revision. *The Modern Language Journal* 78 (4), 484–496.

Guerrero, M.C.M. de and Villamil, O.S. (2000) Activating the ZPD: Mutual scaffolding in L2 peer revision. *The Modern Language Journal* 84 (1), 51–68.

Guo, Q. (2015) The effectiveness of written CF for L2 development: A mixed-method study of written CF types, error categories and proficiency levels. Unpublished doctoral thesis. AUT University, Auckland, New Zealand.

Hardman, J. (2008) Researching pedagogy: An activity theory approach. *Journal of Education* 45 (1), 65–94.

Hedgecock, J. and Lefkowitz, N. (1994) Feedback on feedback: Assessing learner receptivity in second language writing. *Journal of Second Language Writing* 3, 141–163.

Hidi, S. and Renninger, A. (2006) The four-phase model of interest development. *Educational Psychologist* 41, 111–127.

Housen, A. and Pierrard, M. (2005) Instructed second language acquisition: Introduction. In A. Housen and M. Pierrard (eds) *Investigations in Instructed Second Language Acquisition* (pp. 1–26). Berlin: Mouton deGruyter.

Huebner, T. (1983) *A Longitudinal Analysis of the Acquisition of English.* Ann Arbor, MI: Karoma.

Hyland, F. (1998) The impact of teacher written feedback on individual writers. *Journal of Second Language Writing* 7 (3), 255–286.

Hyland, F. (2011) The language learning potential of form-focused feedback on writing: Students' and teachers' perceptions. In R. Manchón (ed.) *Learning-to-write and Writing-to-learn in an Additional Language* (pp. 159–180). Amsterdam/Philadelphia: John Benjamins.

Hyland, K. and Hyland, F. (2006a) Interpersonal aspects of response: Constructing and interpreting teacher written feedback. In K. Hyland and F. Hyland (eds) *Feedback in Second Language Writing* (pp. 206–224). Cambridge: Cambridge University Press.

Hyland, K. and Hyland, F. (2006b) Feedback on second language students' writing. State of the art article. *Language Teaching* 39 (1), 83–101.

Imai, Y. (2010) Emotions in SLA: New insights from collaborative learning for an EFL classroom. *The Modern Language Journal* 94, 278–292.

Izumi, S., Bigelow, M., Fujiwara, M. and Fearnow, S. (1999) Testing the output hypothesis: Effects of output on noticing and second language acquisition. *Studies in Second Language Acquisition* 21, 421–452.

Jin, L. and Zhu, W. (2010) Dynamic motives in ESL computer-mediated peer response. *Computers and Composition* 27 (4), 284–303.

Kepner, C.G. (1991) An experiment in the relationship of types of written feedback to the development of second-language writing skills. *Modern Language Journal* 75 (3), 305–313.

Knouzi, I., Swain, M., Lapkin, S. and Brooks, L. (2010) Self-scaffolding mediated by languaging: Microgenetic analysis of high and low performers. *International Journal of Applied Linguistics* 20, 23–49.

Kormos, J. (2012) The role of individual differences in L2 writing. *Journal of Second Language Writing* 21, 390–403.

Krashen, S.D. (1985) *The Input Hypothesis: Issues and Implications.* London: Longman.

Kumar, V. and Stracke, E. (2007) An analysis of written feedback on a PhD thesis. *Teaching in Higher Education* 12 (4), 461–470

Lalande, J.F. (1982) Reducing composition errors: An experiment. *Modern Language Journal* 66, 140–149.

Lantolf, J.P. (2000a) Introducing sociocultural theory. In J.P. Lantolf (ed.) *Sociocultural Theory and Second Language Learning* (pp. 1–26). New York: Oxford University Press.

Lantolf, J.P. (2000b) Second language learning as a mediated process. *Language Teaching* 33 (1), 79–96.

Lantolf, J.P. (2005) Sociocultural theory and SLL: An exegesis. In E. Hinkel (ed.) *Handbook in Second Language Teaching and Learning* (pp. 335–354). Mahwah, NJ: Lawrence Erlbuam Associates.

Lantolf, J.P. (2006) Sociocultural theory and L2: State of the art. *Studies in Second Language Acquisition* 28 (1), 67–109.

Lantolf, J.P. and Aljaafreh, A. (1995) Second language learning in the zone of proximal development: a revolutionary experience. *International Journal of Educational Research* 23, 619–623.

Lantolf, J.P. and Appel, G. (1994) Theoretical framework: An introduction to Vygoskian perspectives on second language research. In J.P. Lantolf and G. Appel (eds) *Vygotskian Approaches to Second Language Research* (pp. 1–32). Norwood, NJ: Ablex.

Lantolf, J.P. and Pavlenko, A. (2001) (S)econd (L)anguage (A)ctivity theory: Understanding second language learners as people. In M. Breen (ed.) *Learner Contributions to Language Learning* (pp. 141–158). London: Longman.

Lantolf, J.P. and Poehner, M.E. (2014) *Sociocultural Theory and the Pedagogical Imperatives in L2 Education. Vygotskian Praxis and the Research/Practice Divide.* New York: Routledge.

Lantolf, J.P. and Thorne, S.L. (2006) *Sociocultural Theory and the Genesis of L2 Development.* Oxford, UK: Oxford University Press.

Larsen-Freeman, D. (2006) The emergence of complexity, fluency, and accuracy in the oral and written production of five Chinese learners of English. *Applied Linguistics* 27, 590–619.

Lee, I. (2008a) Student reactions to teacher feedback in two Hong Kong secondary classrooms. *Journal of Second Language Writing* 17 (1), 144–164.

Lee, I. (2008b) Understanding teachers' written feedback practices in Hong Kong secondary classrooms. *Journal of Second Language Writing* 17 (1), 69–85.

Lee, I. (2009) Ten mismatches between teachers' beliefs and written feedback practices. *ELT Journal* 63 (1), 12–22.

Lee, I. (2014) Revising teacher feedback in EFL writing from sociocultural perspectives. *TESOL Quarterly* 48, 201–213.

Lee, G. and Schallert, D. (2008) Meeting in the margins: Effects of the teacher-student relationship on revision processes of EFL college students taking a composition course. *Journal of Second Language Writing* 17, 165–182.

Leki, I. (1990) Coaching from the margins: Issues in written response. In B. Kroll (ed.) *Second Language Writing: Research Insights for the Classroom* (pp. 57–68). Cambridge: University of Cambridge Press.

Leontiev, A.N. (1978) *Activity, Consciousness, and Personality*. Englewood Cliffs, NJ: Prentice Hall.

Leontiev, A.N. (1981) The problem of activity in psychology. In J.V. Wertsch (ed.) *The Concept of Activity in Soviet Psychology* (pp. 37–71). Armonk, NY: Sharpe.

Li, S. (2014) Oral corrective feedback. *ELT Journal* 68, 196–198.

Liang, M-Y. (2010) Using synchronous online peer revision response groups in EFL writing: Revision-related discourse. *Language Learning & Technology* 14 (1), 45–64.

Lightbown, P. (2006) 'Perfecting practice'. Plenary talk given at the IRAAL/BAAL Conference, Cork, Ireland.

Lightbown, P. and Spada, N. (2011) *How Languages are Learned*. Oxford: Oxford University Press.

Liu, J. and Sadler, R.W. (2003) The effect and affect of peer review in electronic versus traditional modes on L2 writing. *Journal of English for Academic Purposes* 2 (3), 193–227.

Loewen, S. (2011) The role of feedback. In S. Gass and A. Mackey (eds) *The Routledge Handbook of second Language Acquisition*. New York: Routledge.

Long, M.H. (1981) Input, interaction, and second-language acquisition. *Annals of the New York Academy of Sciences 379* (Native Language and Foreign Language Acquisition), 259–278.

Long, M.H. (1996) The role of the linguistic environment in second language acquisition. In W.C. Ritchie and T.K. Bhatia (eds) *Handbook of Second Language Acquisition. Vol. 2: Second Language Acquisition* (pp. 413–468). New York: Academic.

Lyster, R. (1998) Negotiation of form, recasts, and explicit correction in relation to error types and learner repair in immersion classrooms. *Language Learning* 48, 183–218.

Lyster, R. and Ranta, L. (2013) Counterpoint piece: The case for variety in corrective feedback research. *Studies in Second Language Acquisition* 35, 167–184.

Lyster, R., Saito, K. and Sato, M. (2013) Oral corrective feedback in second language classrooms. *Language Teaching* 46, 1–40.

Macqueen, S. (2012) *The Emergence of Patterns in Second Language Writing. A Sociocognitive Exploration of Lexical Trails*. Bern: Peter Lang.

McLaughlin, B. (1978) The monitor model: Some methodological considerations. *Language Learning* 28, 309–332.

McLaughlin, B. (1980) Theory and research in second language learning: An emerging paradigm. *Language Learning* 30, 331–350.

McLaughlin, B. (1987) *Theories of Second-language Learning*. London: Edward Arnold.

McLaughlin, B. (1990) Restructuring. *Applied Linguistics* 11 (2), 113–128.

McLaughlin, B., Rossman, T. and McLeod, B. (1983) Second language learning: An information processing perspective. *Language Learning* 33, 135–158.

McLaughlin, B. and Heredia, R. (1996) Information processing approaches to research on second language acquisition and use. In R. Ritchie and T. Bhatia (eds) *A Handbook of Second Language Acquisition*. San Diego: Academic Press.

McMartin-Miller, C. (2014) How much feedback is enough?: Instructor practices and student attitudes toward error treatment in second language writing. *Assessing Writing* 19 (1), 24–35.

Milton, J. (2006) Resource-rich web-based feedback: Helping learners become independent writers. In K. Hyland and F. Hyland (eds) *Feedback in Second Language Writing: Contexts and Issues* (pp. 123–139). New York: Cambridge University Press.

Min, H-T. (2013) A case study of an EFL writing teacher's belief and practice about written feedback. *System* 41, 625–638.

Mitchell, R. and Myles, F. (2004) *Second Language Learning Theories*. London: Hodder Education.

Miyake, A. and Friedman, N. (1998) Individual differences in second language proficiency: Working memory as language aptitude. In A. Healy and L. Bourne (eds) *Foreign Language Learning: Psycholinguistic Studies on Training and Retention*. Hillsdale, NJ: Lawrence Erlbaum.

Montgomery, J. and Baker, W. (2007) Teacher-written feedback: Student perceptions, teacher self-assessment, and actual teacher performance. *Journal of Second Language Writing* 16 (1), 82–99.

Morton, J., Thompson, C. and Storch, N. (2014) Feedback in the supervision of postgraduate students: Insights from the work of Vygotsky and Bakhtin. *Journal of Academic Language and Learning* 8 (1), 24–36.

Murphy, S. (2000) A sociocultural perspective on teacher response: Is there a student in the room? *Assessing Writing* 7 (1), 79–90.

Mustafa, R. (2012) Feedback on feedback: Sociocultural interpretation of Saudi ESL learners' opinions about writing feedback. *English Language Teaching* 5 (3), 3–15.

Nassaji, H. (2012) Correcting students' written grammatical errors: The effects of negotiated versus nonnegotiated feedback. *Studies in Second Language Learning and Teaching* 1, 315–334.

Nassaji, H. and Cumming, A. (2000) What's in the ZPD? A case study of a young ESL student and teacher interacting through dialogue journals. *Language Teaching Research* 4, 95–121.

Nassaji, H. and Swain, M. (2000) A Vygotskian perspective on corrective feedback in L2: The effect of random versus negotiated help on the learning of English articles. *Language Awareness* 9 (1), 34–51.

Negueruela, E. (2008) Revolutionary pedagogies: Learning that leads (to) second language development. In J.P. Lantolf and M.E. Poehner (eds) *Sociocultural Theory and the Teaching of Second Languages* (pp. 189–227). London: Equinox.

Noels, K., Clement, R. and Pelletier, L. (2001) Intrinsic, extrinsic and integrative orientations of French Canadian learners of English. *Canadian Modern Language Review* 57, 424–442.

Norton, B. and Toohey, K. (2001) Changing perspectives on good language learners. *TESOL Quarterly* 35, 307–322.

Ohta, A.S. (2001) *Second Language Acquisition Processes in the Classroom: Learning Japanese*. Mahwah, NJ: Lawrence Erlbaum.

Ortega, L. (2009) *Understanding Second Langauge Acquisition*. London: Hodder Education.

Ortega, L. (2012) Epilogue: Exploring L2 writing – SLA interfaces. *Journal of Second Language Writing* 21, 404–415.

Pajares, F. (2003) Self-efficacy beliefs, motivation and achievement in writing: A review of the literature. *Reading and Writing Quarterly* 19, 139–158.

Paradis, M. (1994) Neurolinguistic aspects of implicit and explicit memory: Implications for bilingualism and second language acquisition. In N. Ellis (ed.) *Implicit and Explicit Language Learning*. London: Academic Press.

Peirce, B.N. (1995) Social identity, investment, and language learning. *TESOL Quarterly* 29 (1), 9–31.

Piaget, J. (1974) *The Language and Thought of the Child*. New York: New American Library.

Piaget, J. (1977) *The Development of Thought: Equilibrium of Cognitive Structures*. New York: Viking.

Pienemann, M. (1998) *Language Processing and Second Language Development: Processability Theory.* Amsterdam: John Benjamins.

Poehner, M.E. (2009) Dynamic assessment as a dialectic framework for classroom activity: Evidence from second language (L2) learners. *Journal of Cognitive Education and Psychology* 3, 252–268.

Poehner, M.E. and Lantolf, J.P. (2010) Vygotsky's teaching-assessment dialectic and L2 education: The case for dynamic assessment. *Mind, Culture, and Activity* 17, 312–330.

Polio, C. (2012) The relevance of second language acquisition theory to the written error correction debate. *Journal of Second Language Writing* 21 (4), 375–389.

Reid, J. (1998) 'Eye' learners and 'ear' learners: Identifying the language needs of international students and US resident writers. In P. Byrd and J.M. Reid (eds) *Grammar in the Composition Classroom: Essay on Teaching ESL for College-bound Students* (pp. 3–17). Boston: Heinle and Heinle.

Reid, J. (2005) 'Ear' learners and error in US college writing. In P. Bruthiaux, D. Atkinson, W. Eddington, W. Crabbe and V. Ramanathan (eds) *Directions in Applied Linguistics* (pp. 117–278). Clevedon: Multilingual Matters.

Robb, T., Ross, S. and Shortreed, I. (1986) Salience of feedback on error and its effect on EFL writing quality. *TESOL Quarterly* 20 (1), 83–95.

Roberts, B. (1999) *Can Error Logs Raise More Than Consciousness? The Effects of Error Logs and Grammar Feedback on ESL Students' Final Drafts.* Unpublished Master's thesis, California State University, Sacramento, USA.

Robinson, P. (2003) Attention and memory during SLA. *Handbook of Second Language Acquisition,* 631–678. Malden, MA: Blackwell.

Robinson, P. (2005) Aptitude and second language acquisition. *Annual Review of Applied Linguistics* 25, 46–73.

Rogoff, B. (1990) *Apprenticeship in Thinking: Cognitive Development in Social Context.* New York: Oxford University Press.

Rommetveit, R. (1985) Language acquisition as increasing linguistic structuring of experience and symbolic behavior control. In J.V. Wertsch (ed.) *Culture, Communication, and Cognition: Vygotskian Perspectives* (pp. 183–204). Cambridge: Cambridge University Press.

Rummel, S. (2014) Student and Teacher Beliefs About Written CF and the Effect These Beliefs Have on Uptake: A Multiple Case Study of Laos and Kuwait. Unpublished doctoral thesis, AUT University, Auckland, New Zealand.

Sawyer, M. and Ranta, L. (2001) Aptitude, individual differences, and instructional design. In P. Robinson (ed.) *Cognition and Second Language Instruction* (pp. 319–353). New York: Cambridge University Press.

Schmidt, R. (1990) The role of consciousness in second language learning. *Applied Linguistics* 11 (2), 129–158.

Schmidt, R. (1994) Deconstructing consciousness in search of useful definitions for applied linguistics. *Consciousness in Second Language Learning,* 11–26.

Schmidt, R. (1995) *Attention and Awareness in Foreign Language Learning* (Vol.9) Honolulu: University of Hawai'i Press.

Schmidt, R. (2001) Attention. In P. Robinson (ed.) *Cognition and Second Lanugage Instruction* (pp. 3–32). Cambridge: Cambridge University Press.

Schultz, J.M. (2000) Computers and collaborative writing in the foreign language curriculum. In M. Warschauer and R. Kern (eds) *Networked-based Language Teaching: Concepts and Practice* (pp. 121–150). New York: Cambridge University Press.

Segalowitz, N. and Lightbown, P. (1999) Psycholinguistic approaches to SLA. *Annual Review of Applied Linguistics* 19, 43–63.

Semke, H.D. (1984) Effects of the red pen. *Foreign Language Annals* 17 (3), 195–202.

Sfard, A. (1998) On two metaphors for learning and the dangers of choosing just one. *Educational Researcher* 27 (1), 4–13.

Sharwood-Smith, M. (1981) Consciousness-raising and the second language learner. *Applied Linguistics* 2, 159–169.

Sharwood-Smith, M. (1993) Input enhancement in instructed SLA: Theoretical bases. *Studies in Second Language Acquisition* 15, 165–179.

Sheen, Y. (2007) The effect of focused written corrective feedback and language aptitude on ESL learners' acquisition of articles. *TESOL Quarterly* 41 (2), 255–283.

Sheen, Y. (2010) Introduction: The role of oral and written corrective feedback in SLA. *Studies in Second Language Acquisition* 32 (2), 169–179.

Sheen, Y. (2011) *Corrective Feedback, Individual Differences and Second Language Learning.* Springer.

Sheen, Y., Wright, D. and Moldawa, A. (2009) Differential effects of focused and unfocused written correction on the accurate use of grammatical forms by adult ESL learners. *System* 37 (4), 556–569.

Sheppard, K. (1992) Two feedback types: Do they make a difference? *RELC Journal* 23 (1), 103–110.

Shintani, N. and Ellis, R. (2013) The comparative effect of direct written corrective feedback and metalinguistic explanation on learners' explicit and implicit knowledge of the English indefinite article. *Journal of Second Language Writing* 22 (3), 286–306. See doi:http://dx.doi.org/10.1016/j.jslw.2013.03.011.

Shintani, N., Ellis, R. and Suzuki, W. (2014) Effects of written feedback and revision on learners' accuracy in using two english grammatical structures. *Language Learning* 64 (1), 103–131. doi:10.1111/lang.12029.

Skehan, P. (1998) *A Cognitive Approach to Language Learning.* Oxford: Oxford University Press.

Spada, N. and Tomita, Y. (2010) Interactions between type of instruction and type of language feature: A meta-analysis. *Language Learning* 60, 263–308.

Stefanou, C. (2014) L2 Article Use for Generic and Specific Plural Reference: The Role of Written CF, Learner Factors and Awareness. Unpublished doctoral thesis, Lancaster University, UK.

Stevenson, M. and Phakiti, A. (2014) The effects of computer-generated feedback on the quality of writing. *Assessing Writing* 19 (1), 51–65

Storch, N. (2002) Patterns of interaction in ESL pair work. *Language Learning* 52, 119–158.

Storch, N. (2004) Using activity theory to explain differences in patterns of dyadic interactions in an ESL class. *Canadian Modern Language Review* 60, 457–480.

Storch, N. (2010a) Researching grammar. In B. Paltridge and A. Phakiti (eds) *Continuum Companion to Research Methods in Applied Linguistics* (pp. 205–221). London: Continuum.

Storch, N. (2010b) Critical feedback on written corrective feedback. *International Journal of English Studies* 10 (2), 29–46.

Storch, N. (2013) *Collaborative Writing in L2 Classrooms.* Bristol: Multilingual Matters.

Storch, N. (2014) *Investigating Feedback on Writing From a Sociocultural Theoretical Perspective.* Paper delivered at the AILA World Congress, Brisbane, Australia.

Storch, N. and Aldosari, A. (2010) Learners' use of first language (Arabic) in pair work in an EFL class. *Language Teaching Research* 14, 355–375.

Storch, N. and Tapper, J. (1996) Patterns of NNS student annotations when identifying areas of concern in their writing. *System* 24 (3), 323–336.

Storch, N. and Wigglesworth, G. (2010a) Learners' processing, uptake, and retention of corrective feedback on writing. Case studies. *Studies in Second Language Acquisition* 32, 303–334.

Storch, N. and Wigglesworth, G. (2010b) Students' engagement with feedback on writing: The role of learner agency/beliefs. In R. Batstone (ed.) *Sociocognitive Perspectives on Language Use and Language Learning* (pp. 166–185). Oxford: Oxford University Press.

Sullivan, P. (2000) Playfulness as mediation in communicative language teaching in a Vietnamese classroom. In J.P. Lantolf (ed.) *Sociocultural Theory and Second Language Learning* (pp. 115–132). Oxford: Oxford University Press.

Suzuki, W. (2012) Written languaging, direct correction, and second language writing revision. *Language Learning 62,* 1110–1133.

Suzuki, W. and Itagaki, N. (2007) Learner metalinguistic reflections following output-oriented and reflective activities. *Language Awareness* 16 (2), 131–146.

Swain, M. (1985) Communicative competence: Some roles of comprehensible input and comprehensible output in its development. In S. Gass and C. Madden (eds) *Input n Second Language Acquisition* (pp. 235–253). Rowley, MA: Newbury House.

Swain, M. (1995) Three functions of output in second language learning. In G. Cook and B. Seidlhofer (eds) *Principle and Practice in Applied Linguistics: Studies in Honour of H.G. Widdowson* (pp. 125–144). Oxford: Oxford University Press.

Swain, M. (2000) The output hypothesis and beyond: Mediating acquisition through collaborative dialogue. In J.P. Lantolf (ed.) *Sociocultural Theory and Second Language Learning* (pp. 97–114). Oxford: Oxford University Press.

Swain, M. (2006a) Languaging, agency and collaboration in advanced language proficiency. In H. Byrnes (ed.) *Advanced Language Learning: The Contribution of Halliday and Vygotsky* (pp. 95–108). London: Continuum.

Swain, M. (2006b) Verbal protocols. What does it mean for research to use speaking as a data collection tool? In M. Chalhoub-Deville, C.A. Chappelle and P. Duff (eds) *Inference and Generalizability in Applied Linguistics. Multiple Perspectives* (pp. 97–113). Amsterdam: John Benjamins.

Swain, M. (2010) Talking-it-through: Languaging as a source of learning. In R. Batstone (ed.) *Sociocognitive Perspectives on Language Use and Language Learning* (pp. 112–130). Oxford: Oxford University Press.

Swain, M. (2013) The inseparability of cognition and emotion in second language learning. *Language Teaching* 46, 195–207.

Swain, M. and Lapkin, S. (1995) Problems in output and the cognitive processes they generate: A step towards second language learning. *Applied Linguistics* 16 (3), 371–391.

Swain, M. and Lapkin, S. (1998) Interaction and second langauge learning two adolescent French immersion students working together. *The Modern Language Journal* 83, 320–337.

Swain, M. and Lapkin, S. (2002) Talking it through: Two French immersion learners' response to reformulation. *International Journal of Educational Research* 37 (3 and 4), 285–304.

Swain, M., Kinnear, P. and Steinman, L. (2011) *Sociocultural Theory in Second Language Education: An Introduction Through Narratives (1st edn).* Bristol: Multilingual Matters.

Tafazoli, D., Nostratzadeh, H. and Hosseini, N. (2014) Computer-mediated corrective feedback in ESP courses: Reducing grammatical errors via email. *Procedia-Social and Behavioural Sciences* 136, 355–359.

Thorne, S. (2004) Cultural historical activity theory and the object of innovation. In O. St John, K. van Esch and E. Schalkwijk (eds) *New Insights into Foreign Language Learning and Teaching* (pp. 51–70). Frankfurt, Germany: Peter Lang.

Tocalli-Beller, A. and Swain, M. (2005) Reformulation: The cognitive conflict and L2 learning it generates. *International Journal of Applied Linguistics* 15 (1), 5–28.

Tomlin, R.S. and Villa, V. (1994) Attention in cognitive science and second language acquisition. *Studies in Second Language Acquisition* 16 (2), 183–203.

Truscott, J. (1996) The case against grammar correction in L2 writing classes. *Language Learning* 46 (2), 327–369.

Truscott, J. (1999) The case for 'The case against grammar correction in L2 writing classes': A response to Ferris. *Journal of Second Language Writing* 8 (2), 111–122.

Truscott, J. (2004) Evidence and conjecture: A response to Chandler. *Journal of Second Language Writing* 13, 337–343.

Truscott, J. (2007) The effect of error correction on learners' ability to write accurately. *Journal of Second Language Writing* 16 (4), 255–272.

Truscott, J. (2009) Arguments and appearances: A response to Chandler. *Journal of Second Language Writing* 18, 59–60.

Truscott, J. and Hsu, A.Y.P. (2008) Error correction, revision, and learning. *Journal of Second Language Writing* 17 (4), 292–305.

Tsui, A.B.M. and Ng, M. (2000) Do secondary L2 writers benefit from peer comments? *Journal of Second Language Writing* 9, 147–170. doi:10.1016/S1060-3743 (00)00022-9.

Ullman, M. (2001) The declarative/procedural model of lexicon and grammar. *Journal of Psycholinguistic Research* 30, 37–69.

Van Beuningen, C.G., De Jong, N.H. and Kuiken, F. (2008) The effect of direct and indirect corrective feedback on L2 learners' written accuracy. *ITL-Review of Applied Linguistics* 156, 279–296.

Van Beuningen, C.G., De Jong, N.H. and Kuiken, F. (2012) Evidence on the effectiveness of comprehensive error correction in second language writing. *Language Learning* 62 (1), 1–41.

van Lier, L. (1996) *Interaction in the Language Curriculum: Awareness, Autonomy and Authenticity.* London: Longman.

van Lier, L. (2000) From input to affordances: Social-interactive learning from an ecological perspective. In J.P. Lantolf (ed.) *Sociocultural Theory and Second Language Learning* (pp. 245–260). Oxford: Oxford University Press.

Verspoor, M., Lowie, W. and van Dijk, M. (2008) Variability in second language development from a dynamic systems perspective. *Modern Language Journal* 92, 214–231.

Villamil, O.S. and Guerrero, M.C.M. de (1996) Peer revision in the L2 class-room: Socio-cognitive activities, mediating strategies, and aspects of social behavior. *Journal of Second Language Writing* 5, 51–75. doi:10.1016/S1060-3743 (96)90015-6.

Villamil, O.S. and Guerrero, M.C.M. de (1998) Assessing the impact of peer revision on L2 writing. *Applied Linguistics* 19, 491–514. doi:10.1093/applin/19.4.491.

Villamil, O.S. and Guerrero, M.C.M. de (2006) Sociocultural theory: A framework for understanding the social-cognitive dimensions of peer feedback. In K. Hyland and F. Hyland (eds) *Feedback in Second Language Writing. Contexts and Issues* (pp. 23–41). New York: Cambridge University Press.

Vygotsky, L.S. (1978) *Mind in Society: The Development of Higher Psychological Processes.* Cambridge, MA: Harvard University Press.

Vygotsky, L.S. (1981) The genesis of higher mental functions. In J.V. Wertsch (ed.) *The Concept of Activity in Soviet Psychology* (pp. 144–188). Armonk, NY: M.E. Sharpe.

Vygotsky, L.S. (1987) Thinking and Speech. In R.W. Reiber, A.S. Carton and N. Minik (eds) *The Collected Works of L.S. Vygotsky. Volume 1: Problems of General Psychology* (pp. 37–285). New York: Plenum Press.

Ware, P.D. and Warschauer, M. (2006) Electronic feedback and second language writing. In K. Hyland and F. Hyland (eds) *Feedback in Second Language Writing: Contexts and Issues* (pp. 105–122). New York: Cambridge University Press.

Watanabe, Y. (2014) Collaborative and Independent Writing: Japanese University English Learners' Processes, Texts and Opinions. Unpublished PhD thesis, Ontario Institute of Studies in Education, The University of Toronto, Canada.

Weissberg, R. (2006) Scaffolded feedback: Tutorial conversations with advanced L2 writers. In K. Hyland and F. Hyland (eds) *Feedback in Second Language Writing: Contexts and Issues* (pp. 246–265). New York: Cambridge University Press.

Wells, G. (1998) Using L1 to master L2: A response to Anton and DiCamilla's 'Socio-cognitive functions of L1 collaborative interaction in the L2 classroom'. *Canadian Modern Language Review* 54, 343–53.

Wells, G. (1999) *Dialogic Inquiry: Towards a Sociocultural Practice and Theory of Education.* New York: Cambridge University Press.

Wertsch, J.V. (1991) *Voices of the Mind. A sociocultural Approach to Mediated Action.* Cambridge, MA: Harvard University Press.

Wigglesworth, G. and Storch, N. (2012) Feedback and writing development through collaboration: A socio-cultural approach. In R. Manchón (ed.) *L2 Writing Development: Multiple Perspectives* (pp. 69–100). Boston: de Gruyter.

Williams, J. (2012) The potential role(s) of writing in second language development. *Journal of Second Language Writing* 21 (4), 321–331.

Wilson, K. and Devereux, L. (2014) Scaffolding theory: High challenge, high support in Academic Language and Learning (ALL) contexts. *Journal of Academic Language and Learning* 8, A91–100.

Wood, D., Bruner, J.S. and Ross, G. (1976) The role of tutoring in problem-solving. *Journal of Child Psychology and Psychiatry* 17, 89–100.

Xu, C. (2009) Overgeneralization from a narrow focus: A response to Ellis *et al.* (2008) and Bitchener (2008) *Journal of Second Language Writing* 18, 270–275.

Yang, M., Badger, R. and Yu, Z. (2006) A comparative study of peer and teacher feedback in a Chinese EFL writing class. *Journal of Second Language Writing* 15 (3), 179–200.

Yashima, T. (2002) Willingness to communicate in a second language: The Japanese EFL context. *Modern Language Journal* 86, 55–66.

Yeh, S-W. and Lo, J-J. (2009) Using online annotations to support error correction and corrective feedback. *Computers & Education* 52, 882–892.

Young, R. (1996) Form-function relations in English interlanguage. In R. Bayley and D.R. Preston (eds) *Second Language Acquisition and Linguistic Variation* (pp. 135–175). Amsterdam: John Benjamins.

Zhao, H. (2010) Investigating learners' use and understanding of peer and teacher feedback on writing: A comparative study in a Chinese English writing classroom. *Assessing Writing* 15 (1), 3–17.

Zhu, W. and Mitchell, D. (2012) Participation in peer response as activity: An examination of peer response stances from an activity theory perspective. *TESOL Quarterly* 46 (2), 362–386.

Index